Double Act

Double Act

Ten one-act plays on five themes

Edited by
Mark Shackleton

Edward Arnold

© Mark Shackleton 1985

First published in Great Britain 1985 by
Edward Arnold (Publishers) Ltd, 41 Bedford Square,
London WC1B 3DQ

Edward Arnold (Australia) Pty Ltd, 80 Waverley Road,
Caulfield East, Victoria 3145, Australia

Edward Arnold, 300 North Charles Street, Baltimore,
Maryland 21201, U.S.A.

British Library Cataloguing in Publication Data

Double act: ten one-act plays on five themes.
  1. English drama——20th century
  I. Shackleton, Mark
  822'.914'08   PR1272

  ISBN 0-7131-8269-5

Text set in 9/10 pt Century Compugraphic
by Colset Private Ltd, Singapore
Printed and bound by
Richard Clay (The Chaucer Press) Ltd, Bungay, Suffolk.

CONTENTS

ACKNOWLEDGEMENTS

I would like to thank my colleagues in the English Department and the Language Centre of the University of Helsinki who have tried out these materials in their classes, and have greatly helped with their valuable advice and suggestions.

I am also very grateful to Pat Poussa for her advice on British pronunciation and to Eugene Holman for his help with American pronunciation.

Finally, my thanks to those students from the University of Helsinki who have been the 'guinea pigs'. Their stimulating and useful comments have helped me a great deal.

The publishers would like to thank the following for permission to include plays which are copyright. Please note that all rights whatsoever in these plays are reserved and all applications for performance must be made in advance to the copyright holders before rehearsals begin.

ACTAC (Theatrical & Cinematic) Ltd for David Campton 'Us and Them' (16 Cadogan Lane, London SW1 (Professional) and Samuel French Ltd, 52 Fitzroy Street London W1 (Amateur)); Edward Arnold (Publishers) Ltd for James Saunders 'Over the Wall' (41 Bedford Square, London WC1B 3DQ); Associated Book Publishers (U.K.) Ltd for Lyndon Brook 'Score' from *Mixed Doubles*, Harold Pinter 'The Applicant' and Alan Ayckbourn 'Mother Figure' (11 New Fetter Lane, London EC4P 4EE); Samuel French Ltd for Constance Cox 'Maria Marten' and A A Milne 'The Man in the Bowler Hat' (52 Fitzroy Street, London W1P 6JR); Elaine Greene Ltd for Michael Frayn 'Black and Silver' from *The Two of Us* (31 Newington Green, London N16 9PU); William Morris Agency Inc for Edward Albee 'The Sand Box' from *Three Plays* (1960) (1350 Avenue of the Americas, New York, New York 10019) published by Coward-McCann Inc and N F Simpson for his 'Gladly Otherwise' (9 Horsepool Lane, Husborne Crawley, Bedfordshire MK43 OXD).

INTRODUCTION

Double Act is a collection of one-act plays on five themes. The plays have been chosen for their intrinsic interest and merit, as well as for their performance potential in the classroom. Care has also been taken to ensure that the level of English throughout is one accessible to the higher intermediate student of English as a foreign or second language. The plays are neither abridged nor simplified, and would also be suitable for native English speakers wishing to perform and discuss plays. As some plays are more demanding than others, the plays are graded into two categories: A (no special difficulties) and B (more demanding). The teacher will find that the *Teachers' notes* contain full guidance on how to approach the plays in the classroom.

Each pair of plays is linked thematically. This allows the student to consider the treatment of an idea from two different points of view. The plays are also linked by genre, and this gives the student an understanding of the variety of means dramatists have at their disposal to express their interests and ideas.

Each play is followed by:
1. A *Glossary*, which gives explanations *in context*, and is intended to help the play reader to read fluently and with enjoyment. Words chosen to be glossed are difficult yet essential words which cannot easily be deduced from the context.
2. A series of *Questions*, which are intended to assist comprehension and appreciation. For this reason, a more demanding main question is followed by a series of easier questions which, step by step, help the reader to build up an understanding of the issues raised by the main question. The easier questions are primarily for the reader working alone; the main questions are possible starting points for group discussion.
3. A number of *Drama Activities* through which students can come to an appreciation of the language and ideas of the play, as well as actively expressing themselves in an imaginative way.
4. A section on *Staging*, which is designed to encourage

7

students to think of the play as a scenario for a number of different interpretations. This section also provides food for thought for any group wishing to put on a full-scale performance in front of an audience (see page 6).

Abbreviations Used in the Glossaries

Am.E.:   American English.
Br.E.:   British English.
coll.:   colloquial. Used to describe the kind of language appropriate to informal speech.
dial.:   dialect.
sl.:   slang.

Brief Definitions of Genres

REVUE SKETCHES

A revue is a light theatrical show which contains short comic pieces, songs and, sometimes, dance, but has no continuous story. A sketch is a short comic piece, usually with a small number of characters, which presents a familiar situation from an unusual or humorous angle, or which may, perhaps, satirize current events. It is common for sketches to end in a 'punch line': a line or two at the end of the piece that gives rise to amusement or surprise and may provide the key to the meaning of the whole sketch.

PARABLE PLAYS

A parable is a short, simple story which puts forward a moral lesson or general truth. Parables teach by drawing a moral from events, the truth of the moral usually being of more importance than the characterization of the people involved in these events.

COMEDIES

Comedy usually deals with humorous, familiar events and the behaviour of ordinary people who speak the language of everyday life. Although the main purpose of comedy is to amuse, it may also have a serious or satiric purpose. Characterization is often exaggerated for humorous effect, and it is typical for a comic play to begin with difficulties and end happily.

MELODRAMAS

Melodramas are sensational, often sentimental, plays with improbable plots dealing with exciting and sometimes shocking events. Melodramas were especially popular dramatic entertainments in Britain in the nineteenth century, though melodrama still lives on in some films and television dramas today. The typical characters of the melodrama are the noble hero, the long-suffering heroine and the wicked villain, and the style of acting strongly favours emotional and exaggerated gestures, the focus being not on realistic characterization but on sensational incidents and dramatic staging. Usually the virtuous hero and heroine triumph over the villain in the end.

ABSURDIST PLAYS

The 'Theatre of the Absurd' is a term usually associated with the French playwright, Eugene Ionesco, and the Irish playwright, Samuel Beckett. In their plays, the human situation is essentially seen as absurd, the meaning of life being indecipherable, and man's existence purposeless. The language found in such plays frequently uses clichés and repetitions which give the plays their absurd or ridiculous quality, although their underlying message remains serious. Typically, the action of the plays progresses in a series of images rather than by logically ordered events. Ayckbourn is not an 'Absurd' dramatist and his play, *Mother Figure*, included here, merely contains absurd elements. Albee, however, was associated with the 'Theatre of the Absurd' in his early plays, especially with regard to his use of language rather than his message.

Stage Directions

The following definitions explain words which appear as stage directions in the plays contained in this book.

aside: words spoken by an actor which other persons on the stage are supposed not to hear.

blackout: a sudden turning out of all the stage lights to signal the end of the play, or of part of the play.

downstage (*down*):   the front of the stage.

far stage: at the right or left edge of the stage.

floats: the lights at the front of the stage which shine on the actors.

following-spot: a bright round area of light that follows an
actor as he or she moves about the stage.

footlights: see *floats*.

off stage (*off*):   not on the open stage, out of the audience's view.

out front: 1. in the audience, as, for example: *The actor asked if
there were many people out front tonight.*

2. a way of speaking one's lines directly *at* the
audience (a style of acting typical of traditional melodrama),
as: *The actor delivered his lines out front.*

raked stage: a stage that is sloped upwards towards the back.

spots: bright round areas of light shining on the actors.

stage centre (*centre, C*):   the centre of the stage.

stage left (*left, L*):   to the left of an actor facing the theatre seats.

stage right: (*right, R*):   to the right of an actor facing the theatre
seats.

tableau: pause in which a group of actors neither speak nor
move; scene represented in this way.

tabs: stage curtains.

upstage (*up*):   the back of the stage.

wings: the sides of the stage where actors are hidden from the
audience's view.

TEACHERS' NOTES

Drama has enormous potential as a stimulus and aid in language learning. The plays chosen here use language in a natural and realistic way within a context that is immediately clear and imaginatively interesting. As far as EFL and ESL students are concerned, plays written by native English speakers for a native English-speaking audience have the great appeal of not smacking of the classroom. They have not been written to demonstrate a particular structure nor a particular function. They have been written to make people laugh or think — perhaps both — and yet, quite naturally and realistically, they employ language which foreign learners will need to recognize or use when expressing themselves in English. Pinter and Simpson, for example, use the language of power and reticence, Saunders' ear picks up the cadences of self-satisfied cliché, Campton employs the language of suspicion, Brook and Frayn report with deadly accuracy the things people say to each other when arguing and complaining, and so on. The genuineness of the language and of the dramatic situation are recognized by the student and the imaginative response that follows is immensely rewarding for all concerned.

Another great bonus with plays is that, by acting out a dialogue, students are encouraged to suit the action to the word, the word to the action, to use their bodies and facial expressions, to relate to each other and react to each other's statements and feelings. The paralinguistic aspect of language cannot be taught as such, it must be experienced. Taking the part of Miss Piffs in Pinter's *Applicant*, the student must lean forward to utter her threats, and Lamb of course cannot help but shrink back in fright. Both the body and the voice are working together and this is being done naturally, with a minimum of fuss or teaching — and, of course, it is fun.

Drama in the classroom can also take the student one step closer to the real-life situation. How rarely the unexpected or unpredictable occurs in the classroom, and how often in real life. The improvised sketches in the *Drama Activities* sections of this book go some way towards bridging the gap between life inside and outside the classroom, for through improvisation a student can learn how to respond swiftly and accurately to the chance remark and the unexpected development.

Grading

The teacher who comes to this selection for the first time will find that some plays are more demanding than others, the main potential difficulties being those of linguistic complexity, complex stage directions and cultural remoteness. Bearing these factors in mind, the plays are graded below into two categories: A (no special difficulties), and B (more demanding). A brief indication of the nature of the potential difficulty is given, together with suggestions on how to deal with it. More detailed guidance is given in the sections headed *Suggested Pre-Reading Activities* and *Suggested Post-Reading Activities*.

APPLICANT   *A Grading*

GLADLY OTHERWISE   *A Grading*
Some students may find Simpson's humour and the point of Simpson's play a little hard to grasp. Note that *question 3* draws attention to Simpson's individual use of language, which creates surprising and comic effects. *Question 1* makes it clear that the Man is a representative and not a realistic figure, and that the play is about power and authority.

OVER THE WALL   *A Grading*

US AND THEM   *A Grading*

SCORE   *B Grading*
The difficulties of this play lie in following the stage directions and interpreting the unheard responses in the one-sided conversations. The vocabulary preparation given in the *Pre-Reading Activities* is a help here, so is *exercise 1(a)* in the *Drama Activities*. Some cultural background information may be necessary. Elicit from the students what social class they think the couples belong to. (References to au pairs, Harry and Jim's jobs, dress allowances etc. would indicate upper middle class.) In Britain, tennis is not generally a game for the privileged alone, but this foursome are probably playing on a club court, not on a public court.

BLACK AND SILVER   *A Grading*
An interesting line of discussion might be to compare the roles of husband and wife in this one-act play with those played by married couples in other cultures. Do husbands change nappies in the students' country, for example? If so, is this something

that is accepted willingly or grudgingly? In this play, the roles played by the husband and the wife would be very typical of many young married couples in Britain.

THE MAN IN THE BOWLER HAT   *A Grading*
A brief discussion of some of the conventions of melodrama (see *Brief Definitions of Genres*, p. 8) may be necessary with some groups.

MARIA MARTEN   *A Grading*
The notes given on p. 146 on the historical background to Maria's murder, the British Music Hall, and the importance of audience participation should be read prior to a reading of the play. The whole class can join in with this sketch — those not taking an actual role can participate as the audience.

MOTHER FIGURE   *A Grading*

THE SANDBOX   *B Grading*
The writer's intention will be obscured if students regard this play as a piece of naturalistic drama. The *questions* help by focusing on the representative nature of the characters and their thematic significance. Students could consider which parts of the action are 'unrealistic', but also whether the ideas *behind* them are implausible: grannies are rarely dumped in sandboxes, for example, but the elderly are frequently treated like children. Another demanding aspect of this play is the way in which the playwright manipulates the traditional convention of theatre. Help with this is given in *question 4*.

Approaches to the Plays

Below are some suggested approaches to the plays. They are not intended to be dogmatic, and teachers should feel free to adapt the material as they wish. The *Questions* precede the *Drama Activities* as it was thought that students would appreciate having a firm idea of what the play was about before they tried out the language and ideas of the plays in improvisations. However, from time to time, it may well be a worthwhile experiment to do the drama activities before the questions or even before a reading of the play. Teachers should also feel free to introduce the plays in any order they like.

Suggested Pre-Reading Activities

In order to get stress and intonation correct, students need to understand the situation and the characters' attitudes and relationships, so the activities that precede the first classroom reading are very important. Wherever possible, the plays should be read at home and the students should make use of the glossaries, look up difficult pronunciations in a dictionary, and study the questions.

Questions include those on characterization, theme, genre and language. Probably the most important questions at the pre-classroom reading stage are the questions on characterization. Parts can be assigned beforehand and the questions that relate to those parts studied. In plays which have a cast of only two, students can prepare their parts in pairs outside the class and the classroom session can be given over to comparing the different readings or presentations. With larger casts, the class can be divided up into different groups, each group being responsible for a different character. In the classroom the members of each group can compare their responses and present a consensus of their fndings to the rest of the class before proceeding to a classroom reading.

Whether the class have studied the play beforehand or not, the teacher can prepare the students for the classroom reading by choosing from the following activities:

1. Introducing the playwright and his works.
2. Introducing the genre.
3. Presenting the most difficult key vocabulary and pronunciations.
4. Explaining stage directions.
5. Introducing the main characters.
6. Playing a recording of a short extract from the play spoken by native speakers, or taking a key extract and acting it out in class, for interpretation, prediction and comment.
7. Using the recorded extract to point out some important features of pronunciation, intonation, stress etc.
8. Doing some or all of the *Drama Activities* which follow each play (to help students with their improvisations, the teacher may be required to give a brief summary of the play).
9. Casting the parts (with the longer plays and with plays which have small casts, parts can quickly be swapped around in mid-reading to give more people a chance to read), clearing a space and setting out props.

Here is an example of how this would work in practice, taking the first play, Harold Pinter's *Applicant*.

1. The information can be taken from the introduction on p. 28.
2. Brief definitions of genres are given on p. 8. Question 4 (p. 34) also directs students towards an appreciation of such characteristics of revue sketches as the unexpected twist to a familiar situation and the use of the punch line.
3. See the *Glossary*. Key vocabulary here would be *palms*, *electrodes*, *moody*, *virgo intacta*.

   It is unwise to interrupt a reading once it is in progress, the only exceptions being when an incorrect pronunciation is infecting the whole group of performers or when there is a complete lack of comprehension. To explain all the difficult words from *Edgy*? (p. 30) to *Randy*? (p. 31) would have a disastrous effect on the flow of the reading. The students will understand that, at this point, an interrogation rather than an interview is in progress, so the occasional incomprehensible word is no cause for alarm.
4. The *Glossary* also contains explanations of difficult words relating to stage directions. Stage directions are very important and should not be ignored. The adverbs describing mood and tone should, where necessary, be explained and the lines practised. The teacher can give a model reading of these lines if the student has difficulty.

   Key vocabulary here would be *languidly*, *affably* and *building*.
5. Questions 1. and 2. (p. 34) give help here.
6. From 'Ah, good morning.' to 'Now I plug in.' (p. 29). Discussion could follow the lines of: What will happen next? Why is Miss Piffs doing this? Why doesn't Lamb protest? This isn't a normal interview, is it? etc.
7. Important features here would be a rising tone on questions ('Are you Mr Lamb?'), and a rising or falling tone with question tags ('You're applying for this vacant post, aren't you?'). More detailed explanations are given in the *Suggested Post-Reading Activities* section.
8. All three activities (pp. 35—36) would provide useful preparation.
9. If space allows, several pairs could prepare their own presentations and one or two interpretations could be compared by the whole group. Do not repeat the sketch too many times; this will cause boredom. Otherwise, two volunteers can act it out for the rest (don't press-gang the shy ones into the limelight at too early a stage). Make sure that at the next reading your volunteers are either observers or get only small parts.

Share the parts around. Props: a table stage centre, a chair for Lamb, a high stool (another chair will do) for Miss Piffs. Use of electrodes and earphones, taking objects from drawers etc. can be mimed. The section on *Staging* (p. 37) will help with thinking about the set.

Finally, a word about noise. Noise is to some extent inevitable where drama is concerned, so if you have thin walls, it is best to warn the teacher next door what you are up to. As with parties, neighbours don't mind you enjoying yourself as long as they have been warned beforehand.

Detailed teaching notes will not be given for the other nine plays, as assistance for nearly all the pre-reading activities is given in the introduction to the playwright, the *Glossary* or the *Questions* and *Drama Activities* sections.

Below are notes for all the plays on:

> a) key vocabulary for the dialogue
> b) key vocabulary for the stage directions
> c) key extracts
> d) important features of pronunciation

APPLICANT

a) *palms, electrodes, moody, virgo intacta.*
b) *languidly, affably, building.*
c) From PIFFS: 'Ah, good morning.' to PIFFS: 'Now I plug in.' (p. 29)
d) Questions (rising tone); question tags (rising or falling tone).

GLADLY OTHERWISE

a) *revulsion, washers, recesses, colanders, accomplice, glibness.*
b) *doorstep, booming, at a loss, flustered, disenchanted, asperity, tableau.*
c) From MAN (*off*): 'Mrs Brandywine?' (p. 39) to MAN (*taking ...*): 'Depends entirely on the temperature, Mrs Brandywine.' (p. 40)
d) Questions (rising tone); question tags (rising tone); *how*, *wh*-questions (falling tone); word stress.

OVER THE WALL

a) and b) No special preparation needed.
c) First extract: from N: 'There was once an island . . .' (p. 55) to 1: '. . . Leave it at that. Nuff said.' (p. 56).

Second extract: from 3: 'It's ridiculous.' to 3: 'I want to know what's on the other side!!' (p. 59)

d) Linking; contractions; *wh-* questions; word stress; contrastive stress.

US AND THEM

a) and b) No special preparation needed.
c) From RECORDER: 'How odd . . .' (p. 71) to SPOKESMAN B: '*We* want to live here.' (p. 72)
d) Linking; word stress; contrastive stress; stress time.

SCORE

a) The basic vocabulary of tennis: *game, set, backhand, base line, love-fifteen* etc., *sideline, match, centre line, deuce, matchpoint.*
b) Draw a diagram of a tennis court and mark the movements of the players in a doubles match.
   Stage directions could be introduced here (see page 9).
c) From HARRY: 'Now Jim! . . .' (p. 93) to HARRY: '. . . keep you young!' (p. 94)
d) Contrastive stress; attitude and tone of voice.

BLACK AND SILVER

a) *carry-cot on a conveyor, nappy, Kleenex, Bickiepegs.*
b) *inarticulately, detour, reassuringly, resignedly, gallantry, upbeat, tweedling, peremptory, conciliating.*
c) (With sound effects if possible.) From WIFE: 'Your turn. (p. 107) to WIFE: 'Well, it wasn't my idea, coming back to Venice and getting the room we spent our honeymoon in.' (p. 109)
d) Contrastive stress; attitude and tone of voice.

THE MAN IN THE BOWLER HAT

a) *melodrama* (see p. 9), *bowler hat, I went round in ninety-five, two-seater, waistcoat, Morse Code, Waterloo Station, Paddington Station* etc.
b) *desultory, scuffling noise, sinuous, broods, wistfully, indignantly, spurns, reverie, gagged, sardonically, broken up.*
c) From MARY: 'Did I tell you that . . .' (p. 125) to JOHN: 'Look!' (p. 127).
d) Questions (rising tone); question tags; contrastive stress; pauses; weak forms.

MARIA MARTEN

a) *Music Hall* (see p. 146), *Chairman* (see p. 146), *squire*, *Stage-Manager*, *gel*, *me*.
b) *testily*, *tabs*, *bodice*, *leering*, *reprises*, *minor chord*, *ignominiously*, *in high dudgeon*, *fly-buttons*, *"Nellie Dean"*.
c) From CHAIRMAN 'Ladies and gentlemen, . . .' (p. 147) to CORDER (laughing triumphantly): 'Ha-ha!' (p. 149); or, alternatively, a pause could be made after Corder's entry: CORDER (*as he enters*): 'Ha ha!' (p. 148)
d) Rhyme and rhythm.

MOTHER FIGURE

a) *absurdist* (see p. 9), *dinkie*, *toothipegs*, *botty*, *choccy bics*, *"Georgie Porgie . . ."*.
b) *frail*, *mousey-looking*, *play-pen*, *gingerly*, *sotto voce*, *lamely*, *smirks*.
c) From LUCY (*calling behind her*): 'Nicholas! . . .' (p. 161) to LUCY: 'I don't think I've got dressed for weeks, either.' (p. 163).
d) Questions (rising tone); *how* and *wh-* questions (falling tone); weak forms; linking.

THE SANDBOX

a) No special preparation needed.
b) *whining*, *endearing*, *shrugs*, *calisthenics*, *double-take*, *rumble*, *vacantly*, *mocking*, *mimicking*, *resignation*, *tableau*.
c) From MOMMY (*motioning to* DADDY): 'Well, here we are . . .' (p. 181) to DADDY (*dusting himself*): 'What do we do now?' (p. 182)
d) American stress patterns.

Suggested Post-Reading Activities

The teacher here has a range of possibilities:
1. follow-up work on pronunciation, intonation, stress and vocabulary.
2. a dramatized playreading, including, where possible, sound effects and props.
3. making a sound tape or video recording of the play.
4. writing alternative endings/continuations of scenes; acting these out in groups for comparison and criticism.
5. writing 'parallel' scenes/plays.

6. performing in front of a real audience (for which permission must be obtained from the agents of the playwrights — please see p. 6 for details).

To deal in more detail with each of these points:

1. During a classroom reading, mistakes in pronunciation and comprehension will be made, and these should be noted down by the teacher. Where problems affect the whole class, the teacher can make a teaching point to the whole group, but individual problems should be dealt with by having a quiet word with the student concerned.

Some teachers may wish to do systematic phonological work. Below are some suggestions.

APPLICANT

Questions (rising tone):
   Are you Mr. Lamb? (p. 29)
   Are you a physicist? (p. 29)
   Edgy? Fretty? Irritable? (p. 30)
   Their clothes? Their shoes? etc. (p. 31)

Question tags (rising or falling tone):
   You're applying for this vacant post, aren't you? (p. 29)
The question tag could be read with either a rising tone (speaker checking that information is correct, inviting agreement or disagreement) or falling tone (questioner expects to have information confirmed). Students could decide which is more appropriate here.
   Plug in, do you? (rising tone) (p. 30)
   ... helps to determine my ... my suitability does it? (rising tone) (p. 30)
   Yes, you'd have to, wouldn't you? (falling tone) (p. 30)

GLADLY OTHERWISE

Questions (rising tone):
   Mrs Brandywine? (implying 'are you there?') (p. 39)
   Revulsion? Contempt? (p. 40)

Question tags (rising tone):
   In here, is it? (p. 39)
   Fit the hand, do they? (p. 39)

How, wh- questions (falling tone):
   How are your handles? (p. 39)
   What are they like to look at? (p. 40)

Word stress:

Information-bearing words: that word or those words are stressed which the speaker feels to be most important.

MRS BRANDY-WINE: I've never really *thought* about it to tell you the truth.

MAN: I'm *asking* you to think about it *now*, Mrs Brandywine. (p. 41)

MRS BRANDY-WINE: Oh, yes. I *can't complain*.

MAN: I'm not *asking* you to complain, Mrs Brandywine. (p. 42)

MRS BRANDYWINE: Oh, yes. *Any amount*.

MAN: *Any* amount? (p. 43)

OVER THE WALL

Linking:

Native speakers link words together smoothly and naturally in connected speech. Foreign learners often pronounce each word as if it were in isolation.

Linking is necessary between:

1. a word ending in a consonant sound followed by a word beginning with a vowel sound

    an island   believe it   lived a   better and   had enough

2. a word ending in a vowel sound followed by a word beginning with a vowel sound

    to eat   the old   to each

The Narrator's opening speech provides good practice (p. 55). Students should be careful not to exaggerate the link. This will result in *a-nisland* rather than a island and *to-weat* and not to eat.

Contractions:

The dialogue of the numbered characters up to 'Nuff said.' (p. 56) provides useful practice:

   it's   That's   we're   we've   didn't   There's   humility's

Students should aim for a smooth linking between the contracted word and the word that immediately follows it.

Wh- questions (falling tone):

   What is? Why not? Why not, who says so? Who do you think you are anyway? What sort of trouble? (p. 59)

Word stress:

   You *imagined* it was there . . . (p. 57)

   May I ask what *you* think . . . (p. 57)

... cannot be said to be either *in* or *there*. As for *what* doesn't exist ... (p. 57)

Contrastive stress:

Contrastive stress occurs when an information-bearing word is stressed in order to suggest a contrast:

There's enough nasty *this* side of the Wall, never mind the *other* side of the Wall. (p. 57)

The contrasting idea or word need not actually be spoken, but may be implied:

It still hurts.

You *think* it does (= but it doesn't *really*). (p. 57)

US AND THEM

Linking:

The Recorder's first speech provides useful practice:

How odd   Just a   minute ago   trace of   an echo

come and   wait and   do about   make a

Word stress:

Who are **you**?

We've come a long *way*.

We've come a long *way*.

We want to *live* here.

We want to *live* here. (p. 72)

The words in bold type receive extra emphasis.

Contrastive stress:

We're on *this* side of the wall.

They're on the *other* side of the wall. (p. 78)

Either *they* go, or *we'll* have to go. (p. 83).

Stress time:

English is a stress-timed language, the beats occurring in connected speech at approximately equal intervals. In this passage from p. 75 the stressed syllables are in bold type. Students could tap out the rhythm of these lines before saying them out loud.

Thick enough to stop **cows** from **break**ing **through**.

High enough to stop **chick**ens from **fly**ing **o**ver.

Good walls make **good neigh**bours.

Good neighbours make **good walls**.

SCORE

Contrastive stress:
In the following, a contrast is implied. What is it?
> Better keep my eye on the *ball*! (and not on what?)
> I said his *back*hand! (not his what?)
> There's not a *breath* of wind! (whereas you said what?) (p. 94)

Attitude and tone of voice:
> Sheila speaks *sweetly* (p. 94), in a *cutting* way although still *smiling* (p. 94), in a *dry and clipped* way (p. 97) and in a *mild* way (p. 98).

Looking at the context, try and say these words with the appropriate tone of voice. The teacher may have to give a model reading here.

BLACK AND SILVER

Contrastive stress:
What are the implied contrasts in the following?
> Leave it to *me*! (who does not have to do anything?) *I'll* fix it! (not who?) (p. 108)
> The *Italians* are all right — *they* don't mind him bringing his feed up. (who does mind?) . . . they think he's *marvellous*. (others think he's what?) (p. 109)
> Well, it wasn't *my* idea, coming back to Venice . . . (whose idea was it?) (p. 109)

Attitude and tone of voice:
The tone of the husband when dealing with the baby is described as 'upbeat' and 'tweedling'. This suggests that the voice is pitched quite high and that nearly every word is stressed. What happens to the pitch and stress of the voice when the tone suddenly becomes 'peremptory'? (p. 111)

Ask a good reader to read these passages, and ask the rest of the group to identify the changes. (The tone pitch should lower, and the number of stressed words should diminish.)

THE MAN IN THE BOWLER HAT

Questions (rising tone):
> Did I tell you that . . .?
> Are you sure?
> Does that matter very much? (p. 125)
> Kitchen boilers? (p. 126)

Question tags:
> Did I? (rising tone)
> The first boy, isn't it? (rising or falling tone, depending on one's interpretation. Which tone is more appropriate?) (p. 125)

Contrastive stress:
> *Last week.*
> But she only had it *yesterday.*
> *Boy.*
> The *first* boy, isn't it?
> The *second.*
> The *first* one that weighed seven pounds exactly. (p. 125)

Pauses:
Three dots together (. . .) indicate a pause (see p. 126). What do you think John and Mary might be thinking in these pauses?

Weak forms:
A good command of weak forms is essential for good pronunciation. The main weak forms on pp. 125−6 are printed in italics below.
> Mrs Patchett *had* just had another baby /həd/ (Note that the auxiliary is weakened but not the past perfect stem.)
> I *was* ordering /wəz/
> *the* cauliflower. /ðə/
> going *to* have one. /tə/
> This is the one *that* she *was* going . . . /ðət/ /wəz/ (p. 125)
> They *are* threatening . . . /ə/
> *a* lot *of* /ə/ /əv/
> *and* waiting, waiting . . . *for* something, / ən(d)/ /fə/ (p. 126)

MARIA MARTEN

Rhyme and rhythm:
The rhyming couplets in this sketch provide a pleasant way of dealing with stress time. There are four clear beats to each line. Students could tap out the rhythm before saying them out loud.
> Our **heroine** will **first appear**;
> Her **name's** Maria — so **give** her a **cheer**!
>
> Here's **William Cor**der, the **wicked squire**;
> Please **hiss** and **boo** this **villain dire**! (p. 147)
>
> Oh, **may** my **crime** for **ever** stand **accur**sed,
> The **last** of **mur**ders as it **is** — the **worst**! (p. 153)

MOTHER FIGURE

Questions (rising tone):
  Do you remember?
  All well? (p. 162)

How and wh- questions (falling tone):
  Who are you?
  How are they? (p. 162)

Weak forms:
See Rosemary's speech (p. 163) beginning: 'But then I said to Terry . . .'
  to Terry /tə/
  need *us* /əs/
  to *them*selves /ðəm/
  And that's all right /ən/

Linking:
See the same speech referred to above in *Weak forms*.
  need us   they've only   to ask   we are   by us   put up

THE SANDBOX

American stress and intonation patterns:
The stress and intonation patterns of the more colloquial American expressions are given below. Interestingly, these are nearly all spoken by Grandma, whose speeches are more vivid and colourful than those of the other characters.
  I had to *raise* that *big cow* over *there* all by my *lone*some. (falling tone)
  Will you *look* at you! (falling tone)
  Isn't that *some*thing? (falling tone) (p. 184)
  with this *god(dam) to*y *sho*vel. . . . (falling tone)
  *Lor*dy! (falling tone) (p. 186)

2. Ideas can be gained from the section on *Staging* included after each play. Simple props can be introduced during the first dramatized reading as this increases verisimilitude. Full props are only needed for a performance before a real audience. Sound effects can be recorded by the students themselves, though of course good record libraries will have records of sound effects. Always make as much space as you can in the centre or at the front of the class, move chairs and tables to the side, and make very clear from the beginning where the audience is supposed to be so the students are playing towards a particular part of the room.

3. For those who have the facilities, a useful and interesting experience is for groups to make their own sound tape of the play or a videotape. The recordings or videos can then be compared and discussed with the whole group. Individuals can compare their interpretations, especially where there are differences, and the whole group can participate in discussions of what was successful, what was not so successful, and what improvements could be made.

4. and 5. Exercises of this kind are to be found in the *Drama Activities* sections of the book. Note that the student is frequently given a range of options to choose from. This is useful on two counts: the student will be motivated by being given a choice (language exercises are usually imposed without choice), and there will be welcome variety should the scenes be presented before the whole group. Preparation of scenes and sketches can take the form of either oral or written work. An improvised sketch can be fairly quickly prepared through a brief group discussion, but, if time is available, successful improvised sketches can be written down or extended to form the basis of a more polished performance. Lines can either be read out or, better still, learned by heart.

6. This need not be an inevitable goal, but aiming towards a final performance is a great motivator. Always bear your supposed audience in mind when choosing a play. Do not be afraid to make alterations in the play — substituting, for example, the names of local tennis stars for Virginia Wade and Rod Laver in *Score* will get a far better response from the audience.

Timing

The plays have different running times. *Applicant*, *Gladly Otherwise* and *Maria Marten* last approximately 5 − 8 minutes, the other plays between 15 − 20 minutes.

My own experience with sketches improvised in the classroom is that they should not be over-prepared, and that a short preparatory time (approximately 10 minutes) is usually sufficient for discussion and a trial run before presenting the sketch to the rest of the class. Before the improvisation begins it is preferable for the student to have a clear idea of the role (age, status, job) which he or she has to play, and for the group to have an outline of where the improvisation will lead. Some sort of resolution (such as a punch line, a dramatic revelation, a theatrical exit etc.) is always a good idea.

As a general rule, it is perhaps preferable to spend too little time on an individual activity rather than too much. In that way the class will be eager for more the next time.

The Role of the Teacher

Most input will come from the teacher in the early stages of the lesson, for the teacher has an important role to play in arousing interest and preparing the student for what lies ahead. Once the reading is in progress, however, the teacher can take a back seat. The key roles, of course, should go to the students, although occasionally a teacher might take a minor role. By doing this sparingly, the teacher may well succeed in raising interest and providing a good model. Another way in which a teacher can be discreetly useful is by reading out the stage directions while the play is in progress so that the readers or performers can concentrate on their lines and at the same time get a firmer understanding of the stage action. A teacher could also put him/herself in the position of a student by taking a part in an improvisation with one or two of the class. At the discussion stage a teacher might initiate discussion and then, if possible, keep in the background, or, alternatively, discussion could be carried out in small groups followed by a feedback session with the whole group. Teachers will realise that some of the questions are open-ended, in which case a full response rather than a single 'correct' answer is being sought.

Drama activities involve preparation and thought. Bear in mind likely candidates for certain parts beforehand. Do not be afraid to take a few risks even with a very quiet class. If there is any reticence about acting ability, the teacher should make it clear that the intention is not to produce star performers, but that here is an opportunity for the students to use their imagination and to express themselves through gestures, movements and words. This is, of course, what is required when a student uses English outside the classroom. The teacher's own confidence that drama is a worthwhile and stimulating activity is, naturally, of great importance in establishing an enthusiastic and creative atmosphere in which students can learn not only from the successes, but also from the problems that may be encountered along the way.

POWER
(Revue Sketches)

Harold Pinter

Harold Pinter was born in the East End of London in 1930. From 1949—60 he was a professional actor but since then has only occasionally appeared on the stage. His first play, *The Room*, was performed in 1957 and this was followed in 1958 by *The Birthday Party*. His steadily increasing reputation was established by such plays as *A Slight Ache* (1959), *The Caretaker* (1960), *The Homecoming* (1965) and *Betrayal* (1978). Pinter has great versatility: he has acted, directed, written sketches and one-act plays, plays for the theatre, television and radio as well as screenplays. Pinter's plays have been called 'comedies of menace'. By this is meant that whereas the atmosphere of his plays is menacing — we see people being destroyed by their own inner guilts and fears — the lines of the plays themselves are, nevertheless, often both comic and poetic. Through Pinter's skill, the most ordinary of everyday conversations are transformed into images of great intensity.

Pinter's sketches come from his early period of writing. In 1959 he contributed sketches to two revues, *One to Another* (with N.F. Simpson and John Mortimer) and *Pieces of Eight* (with Peter Cook and others). *Applicant* was published, along with four other sketches, in *A Slight Ache and Other Plays* which appeared in 1961.

THE SKETCH

Lamb comes for a job interview with Miss Piffs and finds it a very different experience from what he had expected.

CHARACTERS

MISS PIFFS: the interviewer
LAMB: the job applicant

APPLICANT

An office. LAMB, *a young man, eager, cheerful, enthusiastic, is striding nervously, alone. The door opens.* MISS PIFFS *comes in. She is the essence of efficiency.*

PIFFS: Ah, good morning.

LAMB: Oh, good morning, miss.

PIFFS: Are you Mr. Lamb?

LAMB: That's right.

PIFFS (*studying a sheet of paper*): Yes. You're applying for this vacant post, aren't you?

LAMB: I am actually, yes.

PIFFS: Are you a physicist?

LAMB: Oh yes, indeed. It's my whole life.

PIFFS (*languidly**): Good. Now our procedure is, that before we discuss the applicant's qualifications we like to subject him to a little test to determine his psychological suitability. You've no objection?

LAMB: Oh, good heavens, no.

PIFFS: Jolly good.

> MISS PIFFS *has taken some objects out of a drawer and goes to* LAMB. *She places a chair for him.*

PIFFS: Please sit down. (*He sits.*) Can I fit these to your palms?*

LAMB (*affably**): What are they?

PIFFS: Electrodes.*

LAMB: Oh yes, of course. Funny little things.

> *She attaches them to his palms.*

PIFFS: Now the earphones.

> *She attaches earphones to his head.*

LAMB: I say how amusing.

PIFFS: Now I plug in.

> *She plugs in to the wall.*

LAMB (*a trifle* nervously*):   Plug in, do you? Oh yes, of course. Yes, you'd have to, wouldn't you?

MISS PIFFS *perches on a high stool and looks down on* LAMB.

This helps to determine my . . . my suitability does it?

PIFFS: Unquestionably. Now relax. Just relax. Don't think about a thing.

LAMB: No.

PIFFS: Relax completely. Rela-a-a-x. Quite relaxed?

LAMB *nods.* MISS PIFFS *presses a button on the side of her stool. A piercing high pitched buzz-hum is heard.* LAMB *jolts rigid.* His hands go to his earphones. He is propelled from the chair. He tries to crawl under the chair.* MISS PIFFS *watches, impassive.* The noise stops.* LAMB *peeps out from under the chair, crawls out, stands, twitches,* emits a short chuckle and collapses in the chair.*

PIFFS: Would you say you were an excitable person?

LAMB: Not — not unduly, no. Of course, I —

PIFFS: Would you say you were a moody* person?

LAMB: Moody? No, I wouldn't say I was moody — well, sometimes occasionally I —

PIFFS: Do you ever get fits* of depression?

LAMB: Well, I wouldn't call them depression exactly —

PIFFS: Do you often do things you regret in the morning?

LAMB: Regret? Things I regret? Well, it depends what you mean by often, really — I mean when you say often —

PIFFS: Are you often puzzled by women?

LAMB: Women?

PIFFS: Men.

LAMB: Men? Well, I was just going to answer the question about women —

PIFFS: Do you often feel puzzled?

LAMB: Puzzled?

PIFFS: By women.

LAMB: Women?

PIFFS: Men.

LAMB: Oh, now just a minute, I . . . Look, do you want separate answers or a joint answer?

PIFFS: After your day's work do you ever feel tired? Edgy? Fretty? Irritable?* At a loose end?* Morose?* Frustrated?

Morbid? Unable to concentrate? Unable to sleep? Unable to eat? Unable to remain seated? Unable to remain upright? Lustful? Indolent?* On heat? Randy?* Full of desire? Full of energy? Full of dread? Drained? of energy, of dread? of desire?

Pause.

LAMB (*thinking*): Well, it's difficult to say really . . .

PIFFS: Are you a good mixer?

LAMB: Well, you've touched on quite an interesting point there —

PIFFS: Do you suffer from eczema,* listlessness,* or falling coat?*

LAMB: Er . . .

PIFFS: Are you virgo intacta?*

LAMB: I beg your pardon?

PIFFS: Are you virgo intacta?

LAMB: Oh, I say, that's rather embarrassing. I mean — in front of a lady —

PIFFS: Are you virgo intacta?

LAMB: Yes, I am, actually. I'll make no secret of it.

PIFFS: Have you always been virgo intacta?

LAMB: Oh yes, always. Always.

PIFFS: From the word go?

LAMB: Go? Oh yes, from the word go.

PIFFS: Do women frighten you?

She presses a button on the other side of her stool. The stage is plunged into redness, which flashes on and off in time with her questions.

PIFFS (*building**): Their clothes? Their shoes? Their voices? Their laughter? Their stares? Their way of walking? Their way of sitting? Their way of smiling? Their way of talking? Their mouths? Their hands? Their feet? Their shins? Their thighs? Their knees? Their eyes? Their (*Drumbeat*). Their (*Drumbeat*). Their (*Cymbal bang*). Their (*Trombone chord*). Their (*Bass note*).

LAMB (*in a high voice*): Well it depends what you mean really —

The light still flashes. She presses the other button and the piercing buzz-hum is heard again. LAMB'S *hands go to his* *earphones. He is propelled from the chair, falls, rolls, crawls, totters* and collapses.*

Silence.

He lies face upwards. MISS PIFFS *looks at him then walks to* LAMB *and bends over him.*

PIFFS: Thank you very much, Mr. Lamb. We'll let you know.

Glossary

The meanings given below are those which the words and phrases have as they occur in the sketch.

Page

29   *languidly*: without energy or emphasis.

    palms: inner surface of the hands.

    affably: pleasantly, in a friendly manner.

    Electrodes: conductors through which electricity passes.

30   *a trifle*: a little.

    jolts rigid: moves suddenly and then becomes completely stiff.

    impassive: without feeling or emotion.

    twitches: experiences sudden movements of the body over which he has no control.

    moody: easily depressed or unhappy.

    fits: sudden attacks.

    Edgy? Fretty? Irritable: easily angered or upset.

    At a loose end: with nothing to do.

    Morose: depressed, unhappy.

31   *Indolent*: lazy.

    On heat? Randy: sexually excited.

    eczema: skin disease which produces red swellings.

    listlessness: feeling of being without energy.

    falling coat: loss of an animal's hair or fur (e.g. that of a dog or cat).

    virgo intacta: without sexual experience (normally applied to a woman).

    building: starting quietly but becoming more and more excited and dramatic.

32   *totters*: moves in an unsteady way from side to side as though about to fall.

Questions

> OUTLINE TO QUESTIONS
>
> 1. characterization: Lamb
> 2. characterization: Miss Piffs
> 3. themes
> 4. language/genre

1. What is Lamb like?

    (a) Is there any significance in his name?
    (b) Lamb is described as *'eager, cheerful, enthusiastic'*. How does he show these characteristics when talking about his profession (p. 29) and when he is given electrodes (p. 29) and puts on earphones (p. 29)?
    (c) Does Lamb always try to answer Miss Piff's questions carefully? Why / why not? Give examples.
    (d) Does Lamb at any point rebel against his treatment? Why/why not?

2. What is Miss Piffs like?

    (a) Miss Piffs is described as *'the essence of efficiency'*. How does the sound of her name suggest this?
    (b) After putting electrodes on Lamb, Miss Piffs *'perches on a high stool and looks down on Lamb'* (p. 30). Why is this stage direction given?
    (c) Give examples of Miss Piffs' questions where she would sound polite and helpful. In which sections of the sketch would she not sound this way?
    (d) Why does Miss Piffs not give Lamb time to answer (pp. 30−31)?

3. What is Pinter attempting to say in this sketch?

    (a) Give examples of questions that would be considered normal in a job interview and examples of those that would be thought strange.
    (b) Looking at the strange questions, what sort of guilts and fears is Miss Piffs trying to uncover?
    (c) What aspects of Lamb's character and of the interview stop Lamb from rebelling against his treatment?
    (d) Is the sketch mainly concerned with the way strong people treat weak people in interviews, or is Pinter's comment more general?

4. How does Pinter express his message?

    (a) At what point did you realize that this was not a usual job interview?
    (b) Why has Pinter introduced Miss Piffs' line 'Would you say you were an excitable person?' (p. 30) immediately after Lamb receives his first electric shock?
    (c) What is the effect of the *'Pause'* (p. 31) after the continuous questioning?

(d) What might the audience be thinking in the *'Silence'*
    (p. 32) after Lamb is given his second electric shock?

(e) What is ironic about Miss Piffs' line 'Do women frighten
    you?' (p. 31)?

(f) What effect do the flashing red lights and the orchestral
    noises have (p. 31)?

(g) Do you find the last line an appropriate and effective
    ending (p. 32)?

Drama Activities

Prepare these sketches in pairs and practise them within your
own groups. They may then be shown to the whole group.

1. One of you is a psychiatrist, the other a patient who has a
    hidden fear that *gradually* comes out during the interview.
    You can either be yourself and choose a fear you have person-
    ally, or can imagine a role and fear for yourself. If you create
    your own role, decide how old you are, what job you do, and
    what type of person you are.

USEFUL PHRASES FOR 1 AND 2

Interviewer (psychiatrist)

You're (name) . . . aren't you?
You've no objection, have you, if I . . .?
Would you say you were . . .?
Do you ever . . .?
Are you a . . .?
Do you suffer from . . .?
Have you always been . . .?
Thank you very much . . .

Interviewee (patient)

That's right.
I am actually, yes.
Oh yes, indeed.
No, not unduly.
No, I wouldn't say . . .
It depends what you mean by . . .
Well, it's difficult to say really.
Well, you've touched on quite an interesting point there . . .
I beg your pardon?

2. A psychiatrist is awaiting a new patient who, according to the report he/she has read, has a deeply hidden neurotic fear (you decide which one). The psychiatrist believes aggressive questioning will always get results. Enter the 'patient'. Unfortunately, this is not a patient — it is Sidney/Cynthia Lamb, who has come for an interview as an accountant and has come in the wrong door by mistake. The interview begins with neither psychiatrist nor job applicant realising a mistake has been made. Develop the situation slowly.

USEFUL PHRASES FOR 2 AND 3

Could you tell us precisely what you mean by . . .
You seem to be avoiding the question/hiding something.
Get to the point, please . . .
Stick to the essentials, please . . .
Could you try and be more specific?
I want a straight answer.
Come on! (indignant)

---

3. Choose *ONE* of the following situations. In all cases, the discovery that the interviewee is not a suitable applicant should emerge slowly.
   (a) Interview a potential spy. The applicant is a foreigner.
   (b) An interview for a student place/lectureship/professorship at a university. The applicant only reads comic magazines.
   (c) Interview a potential bank manager. The applicant has a long criminal record.
   (d) Any interview of your choice where the applicant is clearly unsuitable.

4. Complete Lamb's unfinished sentences, writing in what you think he might say if he were given the chance. Read or act out these dialogues for the rest of the group: have you improved on Pinter?

Staging

How should Lamb and Miss Piffs be dressed?
Where would you place the drawer, the chair, the high stool, the door etc?
Do you think the part of Miss Piffs should be played very aggressively?
If you did not have stage lights, orchestral noises or sound effects, how could the sketch be presented?

N. F. Simpson

N. F. Simpson was born in London in 1919. He worked in a bank for two years before the war, served in the Intelligence Corps and, from 1946–62, worked as a teacher and lecturer. His first play was entitled *A Resounding Tinkle* (1958) and was followed by such plays as *The Hole* (1958) and *One Way Pendulum* (1959). More recently, Simpson has written plays for both radio and television. When asked why he wrote plays, he replied that they had the advantage of containing fewer words. In fact, Simpson is a unique humorist who writes in a style of inspired nonsense. His humour is typically based on carrying logic as far as it will go, and then taking it a little further.

THE SKETCH

A middle-aged couple, Mr and Mrs Brandywine, are sitting comfortably at home. Things soon change for Mrs Brandywine, however, when a man with a briefcase and a loud voice arrives at the door.

CHARACTERS

MR BRANDYWINE
MRS BRANDYWINE
THE MAN

GLADLY OTHERWISE

SCENE — *an ordinary living-room.* MR BRANDYWINE *sits on a backless chair at one side of the stage with his back to the other characters. He is probably over forty but otherwise of indeterminate* age; he is wearing a dark jacket from one suit and trousers which more or less match it from another. A wig conceals a completely bald head. He can be reading a small paper-backed book, but is quite motionless throughout — more like a human doorstop* than anything else.* MRS BRANDYWINE *is a woman in her early forties, whose manner has a sort of surface equanimity* which may well conceal hidden depths of neurosis. She has on a good plain grey dress. She sits with her back to both her husband and the door; she is sorting through a number of what appear to be quarto size* photographs until she holds up one for inspection at arm's length and it is seen to be a full-sized hand print, such as a palmist might find useful. She starts up at the sound of a voice off. It is full of booming* resonance.* It belongs to a* MAN *with a briefcase, who, when he appears, is large and dominant and may well be a salesman. If not, then he is in all probability either a practitioner of psychiatric hypnotism or a trade unionist turned marriage guidance counsellor. Failing this, he can only be a rent collector without portfolio.* At all events he is brisk and in control throughout, and at his most disquieting* when least emphatic. He catches* MRS BRANDYWINE *on the wrong foot at the outset and thwarts* every attempt she makes to regain her balance by tilting* the ground under her whenever she seems to have steadied herself.*

MAN *(off)*: Mrs Brandywine?

MRS BRANDYWINE *starts up. The* MAN *enters.*

In here, is it? Ah — there you are, Mrs Brandywine.

MRS BRANDYWINE *(at a loss*)*: Good morning.

MAN *(tapping the door-handle)*: How are your handles? Fit the hand, do they? More or less?

MRS BRANDYWINE *(hesitant)*: Yes. Yes — I should say they do. On the whole.

MAN: Good. (*He stands back a pace or two from the door and casts a professional eye at the handle.*) What are they like to look at?

MRS BRANDYWINE: To what?

MAN (*glancing up at her*): When you look at them — do they give you any particular feeling? Revulsion?* Contempt?* Anything of that sort? Nausea?

MRS BRANDYWINE: Not in the ordinary way. No. I can't say they do.

The MAN *turns abruptly and crosses to the table uninvited, where he sets down his briefcase and begins to open it.*

MAN: You see, handles are funny things, Mrs Brandywine. You don't mind if I come in a moment — these aren't my outdoor shoes and the sooner I get inside . . .

MRS BRANDYWINE: Of course not. Come in.

MAN: Thank you very much, Mrs Brandywine. A cup of tea would be very welcome if you could manage it.

MRS BRANDYWINE (*flustered* still*): Yes. I've got one outside.

MRS BRANDYWINE *exits.*

MAN: It's nearly four hours since I had anything.

MRS BRANDYWINE *reappears.*

MRS BRANDYWINE: Hot or cold?

MAN (*taking papers out of his briefcase and closing it; without looking up*): Depends entirely on the temperature, Mrs Brandywine.

MRS BRANDYWINE *goes out again. The* MAN *surveys the room, examining handles.* MRS BRANDYWINE *returns with a cup of tea.*

I've been looking at your handles, Mrs Brandywine.

MRS BRANDYWINE (*setting down a tea-cup and saucer, and beginning to recover her composure**): Do you like them?

MAN: Very nice. A present from someone, I expect.

MRS BRANDYWINE: No, not really.

MAN: Keepsake,* perhaps — eh? Former lover? Childhood sweetheart?

MRS BRANDYWINE: Good gracious, no. There's no secret about those.

MAN: Oh?

MRS BRANDYWINE: They were there when we came.

MAN: But how did they get there, Mrs Brandywine?

MRS BRANDYWINE *is brought up short by this question, and keeps a very precarious* hold on her poise* during the following colloquy.**

Two handles on each door — one on either side. They didn't come there by accident.

MRS BRANDYWINE: I've never really thought about it to tell you the truth.

MAN: I'm asking you to think about it now, Mrs Brandywine.

MRS BRANDYWINE: Unless the builder put them there.

MAN: I see.

MRS BRANDYWINE: For some reason.

MAN: What else was he responsible for?

MRS BRANDYWINE: What else?

MAN: The builder. Besides the handles.

MRS BRANDYWINE: Oh. Well, everything really. Oh, yes — he was very good.

MAN (*looking at her*): I see.

MRS BRANDYWINE: Made all the arrangements. I didn't have to do a thing. Doors, windows, ceilings.

MAN: Took complete charge in other words.

MRS BRANDYWINE: Yes. I left it entirely to him, I'm afraid.

MAN: Chimneys?

MRS BRANDYWINE: Chimneys. Roof. Drains. *I* wouldn't have known where to start. But he seemed to have it all organized.

MAN: You were reasonably satisfied, were you? On the whole?

MRS BRANDYWINE: Very much so.

MAN: Plumbing?

MRS BRANDYWINE: Oh, yes.

MAN: No snags* there?

MRS BRANDYWINE: Not that I could see. We had pipes, and outlets for the water. Bath upstairs. Everything — even down to the washers* on the taps. And plugs, for the washbasins.

MAN: He seems to have thought of everything.

MRS BRANDYWINE: Quite honestly we should have been lost without him.

MAN: What did he charge you?

MRS BRANDYWINE: I really can't remember now. I expect he put a bit on the bill — but whatever it was I didn't begrudge* a penny.

MAN: I'm sure you didn't. (*He peers out through a window.*) How far can you see through these windows?

MRS BRANDYWINE: It depends, really.

MAN: What are these? Shelves?

MRS BRANDYWINE: Some are shelves. Some are ledges.

MAN: Getting proper support from them?

MRS BRANDYWINE: Oh, yes. I can't complain.

MAN: I'm not asking you to complain, Mrs Brandywine.

MRS BRANDYWINE: I'm more than satisfied with them, actually.

MAN: Recesses* go back far enough?

MRS BRANDYWINE: Just right, really.

MAN: Not too deep?

MRS BRANDYWINE: Oh, no.

MAN: Nice upright walls.

MRS BRANDYWINE: Oh, yes. They're very vertical.

MAN (*looking round the room*):   I don't see the floor anywhere.

MRS BRANDYWINE: It's under the carpet.

MAN: Making full use of it, I hope.

MRS BRANDYWINE: It's just so that we've got something to walk about on, really.

MAN: What length are your floor-boards?

MRS BRANDYWINE: I'll get a tape-measure (*She finds one in a drawer but never gets round to using it.*)

MAN: Wall-paper? That seems to be missing.

MRS BRANDYWINE: We've had it all pushed back against the wall.

MAN (*looking first at the wall, then significantly at* MRS BRANDYWINE):   Why have you done that, Mrs Brandywine?

MRS BRANDYWINE: It gives us more space. In the middle.

MAN: Space?

MRS BRANDYWINE: In case we have people in.

MAN: What sort of people?

MRS BRANDYWINE: I can tell you better when they've been, really.

MAN: I'd rather you told me now, Mrs Brandywine.

MRS BRANDYWINE: People vary so.

MAN: You could give me a rough idea.

MRS BRANDYWINE: Well . . .

MAN: Total strangers? Friends of the family? Horsemen of the Apocalypse?*

MRS BRANDYWINE: It's hard to say. I suppose some of them might be.

MAN: And the others?

MRS BRANDYWINE: I'd only be guessing.

MAN: Laundry workers, perhaps.

MRS BRANDYWINE: I just couldn't say till I've seen them.

The MAN *goes dubiously back to the table where he sits down to fill in the questionnaire he earlier took out of his briefcase.*

MAN   (*looking up in a disenchanted* way*):   Where are your colanders?*

MRS BRANDYWINE   (*a little anxious to make amends**):   There's one in the kitchen. (*She makes tentatively* for the door.*)

MAN: Plenty of holes?

MRS BRANDYWINE: Oh, yes. Any amount.*

MAN   (*stopping short*):   *Any* amount?

MRS BRANDYWINE: It's choc-a-bloc* with holes.

The MAN *continues looking at her.*

I don't know what to do with them sometimes. (*A little wildly*) I'm falling over them. There's just too many. You don't need all that many. There's no room for anything else.

MAN: You don't know the exact number?

MRS BRANDYWINE: Not offhand.* I'm afraid I don't.

MAN   (*returning to the form*):   Sieves* all letting the small stuff through?

MRS BRANDYWINE: So far, touch wood.*

The MAN *makes one or two jottings,* puts the paper back in his briefcase and seems to relax. His eye as he does this is caught by a tea-cosy* knitted in bright colours. He momentarily interrupts himself to pick it up, comment, and put it down again.*

MAN: Pretty.

MRS BRANDYWINE: Do you like it?

MAN: Attractive colours.

MRS BRANDYWINE: It's a tea-cosy.

MAN: Did you knit it, Mrs Brandywine?

MRS BRANDYWINE: I did and I didn't, really.

MAN: Had an accomplice* very likely.

MRS BRANDYWINE: I wouldn't call it that exactly.

MAN: Why not, Mrs Brandywine?

MRS BRANDYWINE: Unless you call Mrs Prebabel an accomplice.

MAN: What's wrong with calling her Mrs Prebabel?

MRS BRANDYWINE: Oh, nothing at all.

MAN: It's her name presumably?

MRS BRANDYWINE: Oh, yes.

MAN: Not an alias,* or anything of that sort?

MRS BRANDYWINE: Oh, no. It's her proper name. She married a Mr Prebabel.

MAN: Then why are you asking me to call her an accomplice, Mrs Brandywine?

MRS BRANDYWINE: It's just that she helped me with the tea-cosy.

MAN: Oh?

MRS BRANDYWINE   (*becoming a little wild again*):   She held the needles. I looked after the wool.

MAN: I see.

MRS BRANDYWINE: We were in it together, as you might say.

MAN: In other words you were just as much an accomplice as Mrs Prebabel was?

MRS BRANDYWINE: If you put it like that, I suppose I was.

Pause, during which the MAN *looks intently at* MRS BRANDYWINE *before changing course. He closes his briefcase with a snap, takes it up and makes for the door.*

MAN   (*speaking without looking at her*):   Not always very sure of yourself, are you, Mrs Brandywine?

MRS BRANDYWINE: Oh . . .

MAN: Some of your answers could come a little more pat.*

He checks on seeing MR BRANDYWINE *for the first time and goes towards him inquisitively.*

You should try to get a lot more glibness* into your whole approach. (*Looking back at her*) This is new.

MRS BRANDYWINE: It's my husband.

MAN   (*looking him over from various angles*):   Everything functioning?

MRS BRANDYWINE: Oh, yes.

MAN   (*lifting his wig to reveal a totally bald head; accusingly*):
 Except his hormones.*

MRS BRANDYWINE: I've tried everything.

MAN: What does he weigh?

MRS BRANDYWINE: Naked?

MAN: Dressed.

MRS BRANDYWINE: Eleven stone twelve.

MAN   (*trying the chair with his foot*): The chair's taking most
 of that.

MRS BRANDYWINE: He manages on what's left.

MAN   (*about to go*): Is he serving any purpose? Sitting there?

MRS BRANDYWINE   (*wildly trying to be more glib*):   Only to
 keep the floor-boards in position.

MAN   (*in a tone of grave reproof**):   There are nails for that,
 Mrs Brandywine.

> MRS BRANDYWINE *is at a loss.*
>
> (*Going*) You could dispense with one or the other. You don't
> need both. (*Checking*) What are his kidneys like?

MRS BRANDYWINE   (*as before*):   He never lets me see them.

MAN: You could wait till he's gone out.

MRS BRANDYWINE: I don't like to rummage* behind his back.*

MAN: It's in his own interests, Mrs Brandywine.

> *The* MAN *goes out.* MRS BRANDYWINE *turns away bemused**
> *and notices the full cup of tea.*

MRS BRANDYWINE   (*calling*):   You haven't drunk your tea.

MAN   (*off*):   I prefer to see it in the cup. (*More distant*) I'll be in
 touch with you, Mrs Brandywine. As soon as anything
 comes through.

> MRS BRANDYWINE *sits down. She shrugs off the episode and
> is herself again. All the same she is too preoccupied** to
> return to the album.* MR BRANDYWINE *looks up from his
> reading and turns his head to look at* MRS BRANDYWINE, *who
> has her back to him. He turns back and half turns his head
> and speaks without looking at her.*

MR   BRANDYWINE   (*nodding   slightly   towards   the   door*):
 Relative?

MRS   BRANDYWINE   (*returning   sharply   to   the   album   as   she
 answers with unemphatic asperity**):   He didn't say.

> MR BRANDYWINE *returns to his book. The scene is exactly as
> at the beginning. There is a tableau** for less than a second.*
> FADE OUT.

Glossary

The meanings given below are those which the words and phrases have as they occur in the sketch.

Page

39   *indeterminate*: not easily guessed.

doorstop: heavy object used to hold a door open.

equanimity: calmness of mind.

quarto size: large and roughly square (usually 23cm × 30cm)

booming: deep and prolonged.

resonance: re-echoing sound.

without portfolio: without responsibilities, as in the expression 'minister without portfolio', meaning a government minister not in charge of a particular state department.

disquieting: worrying, disturbing.

thwarts: successfully opposes.

tilting: setting at an angle so as to make unsure or unsteady (here, in a figurative sense).

at a loss: uncertain.

40   *Revulsion*: feeling of strong dislike, even sickness.

Contempt: strong dislike, in the sense of despising, looking down on.

flustered: nervous and confused.

composure: calm, control of her feelings.

Keepsake: a small gift whereby the giver hopes to be remembered.

41   *precarious*: not firm or steady.

poise: self-control.

colloquy: formal conversation.

snags: hidden or unexpected difficulties.

washers: small rubber rings inside taps that stop them from leaking.

42   *begrudge*: give unwillingly.

Recesses: spaces in the wall of a room for shelves, cupboards etc.

43   *Horsemen of the Apocalypse*: four agents of destruction riding horses, mentioned in the Bible.

disenchanted: no longer feeling interest, disappointed.

colanders: bowl-shaped pans with many small holes in the bottom, used for draining liquid from food.

make amends: do something to put right something that has gone wrong.

tentatively: uncertainly.

Any amount (coll.): a large number.

choc-a-bloc (sl.): very crowded, packed tightly together.

offhand: at once, without time to think.

Sieves: containers with holes or mesh in the bottom for separating out lumps from food or straining liquids.

touch wood: expression used to keep bad luck away.

jottings: rough notes.

tea-cosy: a thick covering put over a teapot to keep the tea warm.

44 *accomplice*: person who helps another to do wrong.

alias: a false name as used, for example, by a criminal.

pat: easily, without thinking.

glibness: ability to speak easily whether telling the truth or not.

45 *hormones*: substances in the blood which influence growth and development.

reproof: strong disapproval, scolding.

rummage (coll.): try to find something by turning things over and looking in all the corners.

behind his back: secretively, without his knowing (plus, here, the obvious, literal meaning).

bemused: unable to think properly.

preoccupied: fixed on her own thoughts.

asperity: harshness.

tableau: pause in which the actors do not move or speak.

Questions

OUTLINE TO QUESTIONS

1. characterization: the Man
2. characterization: Mrs Brandywine
3. language
4. themes

---

1. Simpson says the Man with the briefcase could be many things from a salesman to a marriage guidance counsellor (p. 39). What type of person does he represent?

   (a) Look at the following in their contexts. What kind of profession might someone have who spoke like this?

'When you look at them — do they give you any
particular feeling? Revulsion? Contempt? Anything
of that sort? Nausea?' (p. 40)

'I'd rather you told me now, Mrs Brandywine'. (p. 42)

'In other words you were just as much an accomplice
as Mrs Prebabel was?' (p. 44)

(b) What do people belonging to these professions have in
common as regards their attitude (sometimes) towards
the people they deal with in their work?

(c) How does the Man treat Mr Brandywine (pp. 44−45)?

(d) Does he treat Mrs Brandywine in the same way?

2. What effect does the Man have on Mrs Brandywine?

(a) What does Mrs Brandywine do as soon as she hears the
Man's voice (p. 39)?

(b) Does Mrs Brandywine complain about the builder in any
way (pp. 41−42)? Why/why not?

(c) Why does Mrs Brandywine try and defend herself
against the Man about the knitting of the tea-cosy
(p. 44)? Does she succeed in defending herself? Why/why
not?

(d) The Man tells her she should be more glib (p. 44). How
does she try to do this (p. 45)? Does she succeed?

(e) What kind of feelings does she have after the Man leaves
(p. 45)?

(f) How does she react to her husband at the end of the
sketch (p. 45)? Why does she react in this way?

3. What is special about Simpson's use of dialogue?

(a) Think of a situation in which the following expressions
might normally be used. Compare their normal use with
the way Simpson uses them.

'I can't complain.'

'It's under the carpet.'

'Making full use of it, I hope.'

'People vary so.' (p. 42)

(b) Rewrite the dialogue between the Man and Mrs Brandywine from 'What are these? Shelves?' to 'It gives us
more space. In the middle.' (p. 42) as though it were
normal conversation between a flat owner and his
tenant. Begin:

MAN: 'I hope the shelves and ledges have been put up
correctly.

MRS BRANDYWINE: Oh yes, they're very good.'

(c) What are the differences between your dialogue and Simpson's?

4. Here are some reasons Simpson might have had for writing this sketch. Do you agree with them? Do you find some more central to Simpson's aims than others?

(a) To have fun with words.
(b) To show how people dominate others.
(c) To get within the official or bureaucratic mind.
(d) To show how easily some people can be dominated.
(e) To show there is a great deal of absurdity in everyday life.

Drama Activities

Prepare these sketches and practise them within your own groups. They may then be shown to the whole group.

1. The Power of Personality

((a) and (b) should be prepared in pairs, (c) in groups of two to four)

(a) Take an object in the room and put it in front of you. One of you should imagine it is something else (for example, a table could become a car). Use mime to show what the object has become. Your partner should try and guess what it is.

(b) Talk about this object to your partner as though you had just bought it and were very proud of it. Your partner is at first surprised (he can see it is, for example, a table and not a car), but the power of your personality persuades him to see it in the same way. Your partner begins to ask questions and sounds impressed.

```
USEFUL PHRASES FOR 1.B

Persuasion

Just look at this . . .
Isn't it splendid?
It was a real bargain.
I'm very glad I bought it.
I'm very pleased with it.
Wouldn't you like one like this?

Doubt

Well, . . .
Mmm . . .
Well yes, but . . .
I suppose so, but . . .

Questions

Will it . . .?
Can it . . .?
Does it . . .?

Acceptance

Yes, I see what you mean . . .
Yes, I'm sure you're right . . .
Does it really?
Well, well!
It's very impressive.
You must be very proud of it.
```

(c) A married couple (A and B) are sitting at home. There is
     a knock on the door. Enter another couple (C and D), who
     act as though they are interested in buying the house. A
     and B look worried, but, overcome by the power of C and
     D's personality, they answer questions about the
     property (tables, chairs, walls etc.) and about the
     builder, and say they have been very satisfied.

     Parts for pairs: A and C
     In groups of 3: A, B and C *or* A, C and D
     In groups of 4: A, B, C and D

USEFUL PHRASES FOR 1.C

Questions about the property

How are your handles/shelves/walls etc?
What are these?

Questions about the builder

You were really satisfied, were you?
No snags there?
What did he charge you?

Replies suggesting satisfaction

We can't complain ...
We're more than satisfied with them, actually.
Just right, really.
Oh no.
Oh yes, they're very ...

2. The Human Doorstep

Prepare this sketch in groups of three or in pairs if the part of
Mr Brandywine is imagined.
   Look at the scene where the Man talks to Mrs Brandywine
about her husband: from 'This is new.' (p. 44) to 'It's in his
own interests, Mrs Brandywine.' (p. 45). Continue this scene
in the same manner, asking and answering more questions
about Mr Brandywine, his appearance, behaviour, habits etc.

Staging

Where would you place the chairs, the table, the window, the
shelves etc? Which pieces of furniture could be left out if you so
wished?
How will the audience see the *'full-sized hand print'* (p. 39) that
Mrs Brandywine looks at?
How can Mrs Brandywine's nervousness and the Man's confidence be suggested by physical gestures?
What sort of voices (high, low, slow, quick etc.) should the three
characters have?

Applicant and Gladly Otherwise:
comparative questions

1. Both sketches are comic attacks on people in authority. Which do you find more effective and why?

2. Do you find the comedy darker or more disturbing in the Pinter or the Simpson sketch?

3. Do you find the endings of both sketches equally effective? Say why/why not.

4. How far do you agree with the following statements?

   (a) In both sketches we do not feel sorry for the people who are treated in a dominating way, because they are weak.
   (b) In the Pinter sketch a particular fear is explored, whereas Simpson deals with fear and insecurity of a more general sort.
   (c) In both sketches language is used absurdly rather than realistically.

CONFLICT
(Parable Plays)

James Saunders

James Saunders was born in Islington, London in 1925. He has a rather unusual background for a playwright, having been a chemistry teacher, who took up dramatic writing as a hobby while studying for a science degree at Southampton University. Like David Campton and Alan Ayckbourn, Saunders has written for and been closely associated with the Theatre in the Round at Scarborough, one of the most important centres for new talent and ideas outside London. Saunders is better-known to London theatre-goers than Campton. His first play for the West End was *The Ark* in 1959, and this was followed by *Next Time I'll Sing to You* (his first West End success) in 1962 and *A Scent of Flowers* in 1964. Saunders has written for the stage, radio and television and his plays range in style from realistic observation to absurdist drama, from comedy to plays of ideas. Among his more recent plays are *The Travails of Sancho Panza* (1969), *Games* and *After Liverpool* (1973).

Over the Wall first appeared in print in a collection of one-act plays from five different playwrights entitled *Play Ten* (1977).

THE PLAY

A Narrator tells the story, and the islanders act it out, of an island with a wall running across it. Who built it, why it was built, or what lies behind it nobody knows or cares — nobody, that is, except one man.

CHARACTERS

Any number can play. But the speeches have been numbered from one to nine. The narration (N) may be shared out.

OVER THE WALL

N: There was once an island, if you believe it, on which lived a people no better and no worse than most. They had enough to eat, without stuffing themselves,* everyone had a day's work (which in those times was considered a great blessing), the old were looked after, as long as they didn't outstay their welcome, and the young were respected as individuals — within reason. All this had been so for as long as anyone could remember, and so they hoped it would continue. For, while they were not exactly happy, they were not exactly unhappy either. And as they said to each other when they bothered to talk about it:

1: If it was good enough for my father it's good enough for me. That's what my father used to say, and it's what I say too.

2: Absolutely. Leave well alone, that's my motto.*

3: We should count our blessings.* It's better than it was in the bad old days.

4: Mind you, it's not so good as it was in the good old days.

5. But things could always be worse. That's what we should think of.

6: They could always be better, of course.

5. But they could always be worse.

7: At least we're allowed to work all day.

8: And we're allowed not to work on Saturday and Sunday.

9: And we've got the vote. We didn't have that in the bad old days.

6: (*female*) *We* didn't have it in the good old days.

N: So they counted their blessings and rested content. Now what made this island different from any other you might have in mind was a wall, which ran across the island a bit more than halfway down and which had been there as long as anyone could remember, and as long as anyone they could remember could remember. For ever, in fact, as far as they knew or cared. They called it 'The Wall', and if they ever talked about it they said things like:

1: There's always been a Wall and there always will be, that's the way things are. It's a fact of nature. There's nothing you can do about it.

2: There must be a purpose in it, that's what I say. Everything has its purpose: wars, walls, it's all meant.

3: There are things beyond us. A higher Wall, I mean Will. Someone's in charge up there. The great Wall-Builder in the sky. He knows what's best for us. Leave it to Him, that's what I say.

6: Or Her.

4: After all, when you think of us — human beings — crawling on the earth . . . I mean humility's called for. It's not for us to seek to understand the sublime purpose.

5: *Of* which the Wall is part.

4: *Of* which the Wall is part.

1: It was good enough for my father, and it's good enough for me. That's what my father used to say. Leave it at that. Nuff said.*

N: So they went on with their business, working as they were allowed to through the week, and on Saturdays and Sundays working, as they were allowed to, at what they called their leisure activities. This wall, now, was not quite straight but curved outwards, so that you could never see the two ends of it together. Not that it had ends for, as the fishermen knew, it continued, when it reached the sea, back along both shores to meet itself again at the far end of the island, so encircling the half of it — a bit more than half.

7: Lor, Jarge, yon Wall goos roit raind the oisland.*

8: Oi knoos thaat, Taam. Tis a well-knoon faact.*

N: So they spoke when they fished. High it was, and smooth, and impregnable,* and how it got there no one knew. There were theories, of course.

9: There is no doubt that it was constructed in the Neo-plasticene* Age by primitive tree-worshippers, to enclose the sacred grove* of the earth-goddess . . .

1: It was built of course, by invading Venusians, as a navigational aid and to protect the space-ships from marauding* dinosaurs.

2: Obviously a natural outcrop of rock, pushed up by volcanic activity and then worn smooth by the wind and rain, an interesting phenomenomenom.*

3: It's a figment* of the imagination. The Wall only exists in our minds. If we stopped thinking it was there it wouldn't be.

N: No one could prove this theory wrong.

4: I walked into it last night in the dark. Look at the bump on my forehead.

3: Psychosomatic. You *imagined* it was there, so when you got to where you imagined it was you walked into it and imagined you hurt yourself. It stands to reason.*

4: It still hurts.

3: You think it does.

N: But since it seemed to make not much difference, if you thought you walked into it, whether you were really hurt or only thought you were, people tried not to. Except for one poor fellow who so convinced himself that the wall was imaginary that he took a flying leap at where it was, or wasn't, and dashed his brains out. Or so it seemed.

5: Excuse me, I'm conducting a survey. May I ask what *you* think is on the other side of the Wall?

6: I don't want to talk about it. I think it's disgusting. There's enough nasty *this* side of the Wall, never mind the *other* side of the Wall.

7: It's like a beautiful garden, with fruit hanging down and bambis* and pretty flowers. And you don't have to wear any clothes.

8: It's like a sort of a ooze,* a sort of — like a — ooze, sort of.

9: Nothing.

5: Nothing?

9: Nothing. Everything finishes at the Wall. Then there's nothing.

1: The fifth dimension.*

2: Ethereal vibrations.*

3: That is to say, beyond the Wall the laws of space-time as we know them no longer operate. Call it ethereal vibrations, call it the fifth dimension, call it a rolypoly pudding* . . .

1: In other words, as far as we're concerned it doesn't exist in there — if one can say 'in there' for a 'there' which doesn't exist and therefore cannot be said to be either *in* or *there*. As for *what* doesn't exist . . .

3: It's like a mathematical point really . . .

9: Like I said, nothing.

2: Don't know.

3: Don't know.

4: Don't know.

6: Don't care.

N: So there it was. Or wasn't, or was in a different way, or seemed to be.

1: Mum!

2: What?

1: What's over the Wall?

2: You wash your mouth out with soapy water!* I'll give you over the Wall! Wait till I tell your father!

3: Dad!

4: What?

3: What's over the Wall?

4: Ask your teacher. What d'you think I pay rates and taxes for? To teach you myself?

3: I asked my teacher.

4: Well?

3: Said to get on with my algebra.

4: Well, then, do what your teacher says.

3: But what *is* over the Wall?

4: The toe of my boot. Get on with your homework.

3: I've done my homework. What *is* over the —?

4: Then do something else. Can't you see I'm trying to watch telly?!

N: Or whatever it was they watched in those days; it wasn't telly.

4: Can't you see I'm trying to watch the goldfish?

5: Can't you see I'm trying to get this ferret out of my trousers?*

6: Can't you see I'm trying to invent the wheel?

7: — cook the joint?*

8: — bath the baby?

9: — darn my socks?

4: — frame a photo of my mother?

5: — write a sonnet?

6: — make a fortune?

7: — get my head out from between these railings?

8: — bury the cat?

9: — dig a well starting at the bottom?

N: Or whatever. And so, in short, on the whole, more or less, without splitting hairs,* broadly speaking, in a nutshell,* they ignored it.

1: Pretended it wasn't there.

N: Well, no, they couldn't do that. Because it was. No, they just . . . ignored it; as you might ignore a gatecrasher* at a party whom nobody knows and nobody wants to, who turns up in the wrong gear* with a nasty look on his face and what looks like a flick-knife* sticking out of one pocket.

3: It's ridiculous.

2: What is?

3: It's stupid. I can't believe it. It's ludicrous.* Here we are with a great Wall across the island and we don't even know why and no one seems to care.

2: It's not for us mere mortals to ask why.

3: Why not?

2: Because we're mere mortals, that's why not.

3: I'm not a mere mortal, I'm a rational human being.

5: We're not meant to understand everything, you know.

3: Why not, who says so?

6: There's enough needs putting right *this* side of the Wall, never mind the *other* side of the Wall.

7: Get on with your work and think yourself lucky. Thinking about the Wall won't do you any good.

8: Do some leisure activities, take your mind off it. Do some healthy outdoor pursuits.

4: All you do is talk about the Wall. Wall, Wall, Wall, that's all I get from you.

2: Leave wall alone, I mean leave well alone, that's my advice.

1: Ignorance was good enough for your father and it ought to be good enough for you.

4: Who do you think you are anyway? God or somebody?

3: I want to know what's on the other side!!

5: Next please. Well, now, what seems to be the matter with you?

3: I'm having a bit of trouble, doctor.

5: What sort of trouble? Stick out your tongue.

3: It'th athout the Thall . . .

5: Put your tongue in.

3: It's about the Wall. All I want to know . . .

5: Bowel movements* all right?

3: Yes, thanks. All I want to know is what's on the other side, that seems reasonable enough to me, only —

5: Sleeping all right, are you? Getting the old* beauty sleep?

3: I dream about walls. Only no one else seems to be bothered, only me, so I —

5: How's your sex-life? Sex-life all right, is it? The old nudge nudge wink wink?*

3: I'm not bothered, thanks. So I wondered if there's something wrong with me, or if in fact —

5: Eating all right, are you? Getting the old nosh* down?

3: Yes, I'm eating. Or if in fact it's that there's something wrong with everybody else. And it's turning into a bit of —

5: How's the pains in the leg? Pains in the leg all right?

3: They're fine. Into a bit of an obsession. Because, I mean, you don't just ignore something like that, I mean I'm not a mere mortal I'm a rational human being and it could be important, I mean, *look* at the flaming* thing, I mean *look* at it, there it is, look, there!

5: Any neuralgia,* headache, backache, loss of breath, vomiting, congenital idiocy, piles, trouble with the water-works, spots before the eyes, dizzy spells?

3: D — I — Z — Z —

5: Falling hair, loss of weight, gain of weight, tenseness, got a drink problem have you, smoking too much, hallucinations, palpitations, eructations, on drugs are you, can you read the top line, overdoing it at work perhaps, worrying about the work, about the spouse, about where to go for your holiday, about the mortgage, about the value of the pound, about the political situation, about your old mother, about the kids, kids playing you up are they, not doing well at school, got a drink problem have they, smoking, on drugs are they, suffering from loss of weight, falling hair, got any worries have you?

3: Yes!

5: Have you seen a priest?

3: Yes. She didn't know either.

5: Didn't know what? They're not supposed to know, they're supposed to give comfort. Seen a psychiatrist, have you, consulted a shrink?*

3: He said it was my mother.

5: Well there you are. Here's a prescription. Take some four

times a day, and if there's any left over rub it on your chest.
Or your mother's chest. I don't care.

3: What's wrong with me, doctor?

5: You're a nut.* Get out, you're wasting my time.

N: So out he got, this nut, taking his obsession with him, and
the doctor turned thankfully to the next patient, a nice
simple case who'd put his thumb out trying to plant beans in
hard ground.

5: Put your thumb out, have you? How's your bowel movements? Sleeping all right?

3: I'm going to start an Association for Investigating The
Wall In Order To See What's On The Other Side. The AFIT-
WIOTSWOTOS. Catchy title. They'll flock to join. Then
we'll get somewhere.

N: But they didn't. And after a while he disbanded the association, with the full agreement of the members — himself.
But he didn't give up.

3: All right. I'm on my own. So be it. But I'm going to find out
what's on the other side of That Wall. If it kills me.

N: And for the next thirty or forty years he did nothing but
think about the Wall. He read books, consulted sages,* took
measurements, drew diagrams, worked out theories,
studied history, biology, theology, psychology, astrology,
cogitated, meditated and did a bit of yoga on the side. He
lost his friends of course.

6: Oh, don't invite *him*. He'll only talk about the Wall.

N: His marriage went for a Burton.*

4: Wall, Wall, Wall, nothing but Wall! I'm sick of Wall! And
I'm sick of you too! I'm going home to father!

N: Slam. His kids turned delinquent.*

7: What are you doing tonight?

8: Thought I'd cripple a few fuzz.*

7: We did that last night.

N: Until finally, old, alone and penniless, he decided on the
direct approach, and built his great invention: a sort of a
catapult, quite novel in those times, which could hurl an
object, or a person, up to an enormous height. He tried it on
a rock, which disappeared into the blue, and then, one day,
surrounded by curious bystanders, sat his own skinny,
threadbare* old body where the rock had been.

3: Wind it up, then.

N: They did.

3: When I say three, pull the lever. One ... two ... thr ... ooww!

N: They did, only too glad to get rid of this nut, this disruptive* influence, so they could get back to watching their goldfish and planting their beans.

9: There he goes!

1: Look at his rags flapping!

2: Bald head glinting in the sun!

4: Better than fireworks!

5: Coo!

N: Up he went, up, up, up, until looking down ... we surmise* ... he saw the whole gold of that sunny day, the whole spread of the earth and seas, saw the tiny moving figures of people and the infinite distances of space. And it looked good.

3: I'm up! I'm over! I can see! I can see over! It's ... It's ... It's ... Aaah!

N: A heart attack — we surmise. But in any case he was too far away for those on the ground to hear him. And as he dwindled into what seemed like a mathematical point, and disappeared, those on the ground shook their heads, or giggled, and went back to their beans, and their goldfish.

Glossary

The meanings given below are those which the words and phrases have as they occur in the play.

Page
55   *stuffing themselves*:   eating more than they needed.

motto: saying that guides me in the way I behave and live.

count our blessings: remember the good things in our lives.

56   *Nuff said (coll.)*:   enough said (there is no need to say anything more).

Lor, Jarge, yon Wall goos roit raind the oisland: Lord, George, that wall goes right round the island (suggestive of dialectal speech in country areas of the south west of England).

Oi knoos thaat, Taam. Tis a well-knoon faact: I know that, Tom. It's a well-known fact.

impregnable: could not be crossed over or broken down.

Neo-plasticene: invented word suggesting a geological era in the distant past. (Plasticene is a type of coloured modelling clay used by children!)

grove: a group of trees forming a centre of worship.

marauding: attacking.

57   *phenomenomenom*:   the speaker wishes to say 'phenomenon', but either does not know the word, or cannot pronounce it properly.

figment: invention.

It stands to reason: it is logical or obvious.

bambis: deer (after Walt Disney's film *Bambi*).

ooze: soft, runny mud.

fifth dimension: two steps beyond ordinary experience.

Ethereal vibrations: heavenly sounds.

rolypoly pudding: a heavy jam pudding, popular in Britain.

58   *wash your mouth out with soapy water*:   said to children who use bad language.

ferret out of my trousers: a traditional sport in some country districts of Britain is to see how long you can keep a ferret (a small rabbit-catching animal) inside your trousers!

joint: a large piece of meat.

59   *splitting hairs*:   worrying about unimportant differences.

in a nutshell: briefly.

gatecrasher: uninvited guest.

gear (sl.): clothes.

flick-knife: a knife with a blade that springs out when a button is pressed.

ludicrous: ridiculous, absurd.

Bowel movements: the passing of solid waste matter from the body.

60 *the old (coll.)*: used as an expression of affection or familiarity (the doctor is trying to sound friendly).

nudge nudge wink wink: when people talk humorously about sex they sometimes nudge (gently elbow) each other and wink.

nosh (Br.E., sl.): food.

flaming: a mild swear word.

neuralgia etc.: the following is a list of common medical problems.

shrink (sl.): psychiatrist.

61 *nut (sl.)*: madman.

sages: wise men.

went for a Burton (Br.E., sl.): was destroyed.

turned delinquent: began breaking the law.

fuzz (sl.): policemen.

threadbare: worn thin.

62 *disruptive*: causing difficulties.

surmise: suppose.

Questions

OUTLINE TO QUESTIONS

1. and 2. characterization: the islanders
3. theme/characterization: parents and children (p. 58)
4. theme/characterization: doctor and patient (pp. 59–61)
5. theme
6. genre

---

1. What sort of attitudes do the islanders have to life and experience?

    (a) Judging from the Narrator's opening speech (p. 55), could the islanders be said to hold extreme or strong-minded views?

(b) Why does the Narrator introduce the comments of the islanders by saying 'And as they said to each other when they bothered to talk about it' (p. 55)?

(c) Judging from the islanders' comments ('If it was good enough ... the bad old days.' p. 55), do most of the islanders agree with each other? Are they satisfied with life?

(d) Are the islanders' reactions to the Wall (p. 56) similar to their reactions to life in general? Do they accept or question the existence of the Wall?

(e) Judging from the first sentence of the play, is the playwright suggesting that the islanders are unique or typical of people in general?

2. Does the playwright succeed in giving definite personalities and identities to his numbered characters?

(a) What makes the comments of the two fishermen (numbers 7 and 8, p. 56) amusing and different?

(b) Four characters have theories about the origin of the Wall (pp. 56—57). Identify by number the philosopher, the astrologist, the geographer and the archeologist.

(c) What sort of personalities do 6, 7 and 8 have as shown by their answers to the man conducting the survey (p. 57)?

(d) How do most people respond to the survey (pp. 57—58)? In your own experience, are these reactions relatively common? Where else in the play have you come across similar reactions?

3. What does the dialogue between parents and their children (p. 58) add to the play?

(a) Who is more curious about what is over the Wall, children or their parents (p. 58)? Why?

(b) Are the activities which the adults say they are engaged in useful or useless tasks (p. 58)? Do you think the adults really are busy?

(c) How do the parents' reactions to their children explain the fact that there is only one adult on the island who wants to know what is over the Wall?

4. What does the dialogue between the doctor and his patient (pp. 59—61) add to the play?

(a) How does the doctor appear friendly? In what ways does he show his real character?

    (b)   How does the doctor treat all his patients? (p. 61)

    (c)   The patient, character number 3, has also seen two other people whose job it is to help others (p. 60). Who were they? Did they give any more help than the doctor?

    (d)   Are the doctor's reactions to character 3 similar to those of people in general on the island?

5.   Are we expected to take character 3's need to know what is over the Wall as heroic or foolish?

    (a)   What effect does this desire have on those around him? (p. 60)

    (b)   Is the Narrator's description of the world seen from the air (p. 62) a beautiful and moving description? Does the Narrator say that character 3 actually saw this sight?

    (c)   Note the reactions of those on the ground to the disappearance of character 3 (p. 62). Are these reactions ones you respect or do you reject them as being superficial and childish?

    (d)   Contrast character 3's attitude to the Wall with the attitudes of the islanders (see question 1.), parents and the doctor. Which attitudes do you admire more, and why?

6.   *Over the Wall* has been called 'a parable of our time'. What features of the play show it to be more concerned with making a universal comment on people's attitudes than dealing with a particular person, time or place?

    (a)   The play begins 'There was once an island.' What other types of story have similar beginnings? Why begin a play like this?

    (b)   Why does the playwright use numbers rather than names and characters?

    (c)   Consider this excerpt:
            4: '. . . Can't you see I'm trying to watch telly?!
            N: Or whatever it was they watched in those days; it wasn't telly.' (p. 58)
       Why mention the television and then say it was not invented? Is the play written about the past or the present or set in a state of timelessness?

    (d)   What do you think is most important in the play — the plot (what happens), the characters (who does what) or the theme (what the play means)?

Drama Activities

1. Acceptance and strong disagreement

Prepare this exercise in pairs.

Below is a list of six propositions. For each item put a tick (✓) in the box that most closely represents your view. See if you and your partner disagree on any point.

	Agree	Disagree
The present exam system [at schools/ universities] is satisfactory.		
The present social services are satisfactory.		
Things are better than they used to be.		
People are happier today than they were.		
People don't have to work so hard today.		
There was more violence in the past than there is today.		

Imagine that you and a friend are arguing about one of these propositions. The student who supports the proposition should use the phrases of acceptance given below (they are taken from *Over the Wall* and make the speeches sound rather self-satisfied) and the other student should use the phrases of strong disagreement. If you wish to adopt a role, decide on your age, what type of person you are etc.

USEFUL PHRASES FOR 1

Acceptance

We should count our blessings.
It's better than it was in the bad old days.
But things could always be worse.
At least we're allowed to . . .
It's a fact of nature.
There's nothing you can do about it.
They/he/she know(s) what's best for us.

> USEFUL PHRASES FOR 1
>
> *Strong disagreement*
>
> I don't agree at all, what about . . .
> How can you say that . . .?
> You don't believe that, do you?
> Never! Look at . . .
> Nonsense!
> You must be joking!

2. Problems and the non-conformist

Choose *ONE* of these situations. Prepare a sketch and practise it within your own group. It may then be shown to the whole group.

(a) Prepare this sketch in groups of three.
     A married couple go to a marriage guidance counsellor. One member of the couple thinks the other is behaving strangely, unreasonably or suspiciously and gives reasons for the opinion. The other member disagrees and feels the blame falls elsewhere. The marriage guidance counsellor should offer advice, which can either be accepted or rejected by the couple.

(b) Prepare this sketch in groups of either three or four.
     A teacher asks the parent or parents of a child to come to the school and complains about the child's behaviour, giving examples of bad behaviour. The schoolchild disagrees and feels the blame should go elsewhere (it could be the parents' fault, for example). The parent/s can either blame the child or the school. After listening to the parents and the child, the teacher should offer advice, which can either be accepted or rejected.

Things to think about

What is your attitude: polite/impolite/formal/informal/pleasant/friendly/unfriendly?
How long have you been married/been at school?
Is this the first visit to the marriage guidance counsellor/the school?
What is your social background? Is it the same as that of the marriage guidance counsellor/the teacher?

USEFUL PHRASES FOR 2

Openers

I'd like to speak to you about ...
Could you help us with this problem? You see ...
I wonder if you could help us? You see ...

Responses

Hmm.   Yes.   Really?   Uh huh.

Development

I feel he/she is being very unreasonable ...
But he/she is quite impossible ...
Not only does he/she ... but he/she also ...

Counter-argument

Oh, I don't know about that ...
I don't think that's fair ...
But what about you ...?

Advice

Well what I really think you should do ...
This is a tricky problem, but ...
You might consider ...

Staging

How many characters would you have? An equal number of male and female actors?
Should the narration be shared or left to one person?
Would you organise the actors into mobile groups or would they all stay in fixed positions (on small platforms or boxes, for example)?
What is happening to the other characters when the Narrator is speaking?
Would you have the Narrator in his own special lighted area?
Which scenes could be emphasized by acting them out in different areas of the stage and lighting up the acting area?
Would you use props?
Would you construct a Wall?
How would you direct the scene at the end of the play (p. 62) where character 3 is flying through the air?

David Campton

David Campton was born in 1924 in Leicester, where he still lives. He became a full-time dramatist in 1956 and, like James Saunders and Alan Ayckbourn, developed as a playwright with the Theatre in the Round at Scarborough, a seaside town in the north of England. Since *The Lunatic View*, performed in 1957, he was written something for this theatre each year, and has also acted with the company both at Scarborough and on tour from 1957−63. He has written a large number of plays, nearly all one-act, ranging, in his own words, from 'domestic comedy, through costume melodrama to comedy of menace'. Campton's plays have rarely appeared in London, with the result that he is not as well-known as he deserves to be. A talented dramatist with a gift for 'serious comedy', Campton is particularly aware of the threat of the Bomb and his vision of people as helpless puppets trapped in frightening situations is a dominant image in his work. Among his better-known plays are *The Laboratory* (1955), *Mutatis Mutandis* (1960) and *The Life and Death of Almost Everybody* (1970). *Us and Them* was first published in 1977.

THE PLAY

Under the eyes of an all-seeing Recorder, two groups meet. They divide the land, first with a line, then with a wall. From there on the trouble begins.

CHARACTERS

RECORDER
SPOKESMAN A
SPOKESMAN B
OTHER As
OTHER Bs

PRODUCTION NOTE

This play was written to be performed by a company of almost any size, of any age, and of either sex. The number against a character (A1, B2) is intended to indicate who makes a statement, asks a question, replies, or interjects, but the dialogue should be shared among the whole company. That is to say, although an A1 character should not speak B2 lines, there can be any number of A1 characters.

However, because the lines have been shorn of characterizing devices, the characters should not be treated as featureless machines. They are people. Character should be projected on to the lines (which is a reversal of the usual process).

The effect to aim at is of one conversation, emphasizing the fact that there is no difference between the people on either side of the wall. They are really part of one group.

US AND THEM

A bare stage. The RECORDER *enters with a large book and pen. He looks around.*

RECORDER: How odd. I felt sure there was someone here. Just a minute ago. There's still the trace of an echo. I could have been mistaken, though. They come and go. . . . Well, it's my job to wait and see. (*He makes himself comfortable.*) I may have to wait some time. . . . But there's nothing I can do about that. Time passes. (*Pause.*) Listen. Footsteps coming from this direction. And more footsteps coming from that direction. Something is about to happen. I must make a note.

Parties A and B enter from opposite sides. They pause wearily.

'Party A from the East. Party B from the West. Worn out* with travelling they come to rest.' (*He ponders* over the last note.*) Verse in an official record? (*He crosses out the last words.*) 'At first they are too exhausted for words.' . . . That's better. 'Gradually they look around them, at first critically, then with growing admiration and delight. But too taken with* their own concerns to notice the other group.'

A1: Here?
B1: Here.
A1: It's a good place.
B1: Yes, it's a good place.
A2: Better than any other place we've seen.
B2: It's a good place all right.
A1: To pause at.
B1: To stay at.
A2: To make our own.
B2: For ever and ever.
A1: This is our place.
B1: Ours.
A2: Ours.
B2: We took long enough to find it.

A3: It was a long journey.

B3: But it was worth every day we searched.

A1: It was worth every mile we tramped.*

B1: Look at it.

A2: Just look.

B2: Look here.

A3: Look there.

B3: Look.

A1: Look.

They point out things that please them.

RECORDER: Of course, they could have commented on the natural advantages of the place — such as the average hours of sunshine, the mean* rainfall, the geological structure, the chemistry of the topsoil, and the lush pasturage.* They'll find the words in time. But next they notice each other.

From pointing out the delights of the place, the parties point to each other.

A1: Look.

B1: Look.

A2: Look!

B2: Look!!

The groups chatter excitedly among themselves.

RECORDER: Party A goes into a huddle,* looking warily* at Party B. Party B goes into a huddle, looking warily at Party A. Nothing to comment on there. It's the usual pattern. Any minute now the Spokesmen will face up to each other.

A SPOKESMAN *from Party B steps forward.*

SPOKESMAN B: Who are you?

A SPOKESMAN *from Party A steps forward.*

SPOKESMAN A: Who are *you*?

SPOKESMAN B: We've come a long way.

SPOKESMAN A: *We've* come a long way.

The SPOKESMEN *return to their groups for quick conferences. After a few seconds they face each other again.*

SPOKESMAN A: We want to live here.

SPOKESMAN B: *We* want to live here.

The SPOKESMEN *return to their groups for quick conferences. After a few seconds they face each other again.*

SPOKESMAN B: We won't let you drive us away.
SPOKESMAN A: We don't want to drive you away.

The SPOKESMEN *return to their groups for conferences.*

RECORDER: One man, one vote. It takes time, but that's Democracy. There's no guarantee that they'll come to the right decision in the end, but that's Democracy, too. Not that I'm complaining about Democracy. It encourages a sense of responsibility. In theory, anyway.

The SPOKESMEN *turn and face each other.*

SPOKESMAN A: Isn't there enough room for all of us?
SPOKESMAN B: There's enough room for everybody.
SPOKESMAN A: You could have all you see from there to here.
SPOKESMAN B: You could have all you see from here to there.
SPOKESMAN A: Agreed?
SPOKESMAN B: Agreed.

The As and Bs shout 'Agreed'. The SPOKESMEN *shake hands.*

SPOKESMAN A: Do you mind if we pause in negotiations?*
SPOKESMAN B: For a conference?
SPOKESMAN A: Agreed.

They go into conference again.

RECORDER: Proposals,* counter-proposals, resolutions, amendments, points of order, appeals to the chair, motions, votes, polls, divisions, objections, and recounts. Everybody has a say. It can become tedious, but it has one advantage — if anything goes wrong, everyone is to blame.

SPOKESMAN A: We have come to a conclusion.
SPOKESMAN B: A conclusion is a good thing to come to. We have reached an agreement.
SPOKESMAN A: It's always as well to reach an agreement.
SPOKESMAN B: That you take that stretch of country with all its natural amenities,* grazing rights,* water rights, hunting rights, fishing rights, arable land, and mineral deposits.
SPOKESMAN A: And that you take that stretch of land with all its natural amenities, etcetera, etcetera, etcetera.

SPOKESMAN B: Furthermore . . .

SPOKESMAN A: Furthermore?

SPOKESMAN B: Yes, furthermore. For the benefit of all concerned . . .

SPOKESMAN A: Does that include us?

SPOKESMAN B: It includes everybody. That a line be drawn.

RECORDER (*musing* * *aloud*): A line?

SPOKESMAN B: A line. That a line be drawn to mark the place where your land ends and ours begins.

SPOKESMAN A: Ah, yes. I was just about to add that a line be drawn to mark the place where our land ends and yours begins.

SPOKESMAN B: Good fences make good neighbours.*

SPOKESMAN A: Good neighbours make good fences.

SPOKESMAN B: Shall we mark it now?

SPOKESMAN A: Why not?

SPOKESMAN B: Chalk?

SPOKESMAN A: String.

> SPOKESMAN A *produces a length of string and the two groups join forces in surveying the ground, and pegging out* * *the string in a straight line. Everyone has his own idea how the job should be done, but eventually it is finished.*

RECORDER: I don't know who gave me this job. I seem to have been doing it as long as I can remember. Not that I'm complaining — someone has to do it. The record has to be kept. Who knows — one day someone may learn from it.

> *The groups stand back and admire their handiwork.*

SPOKESMAN A: It's a good line.

SPOKESMAN B: Though I say it myself.

A1: I don't know.

SPOKESMAN A: Are you criticizing this line?

SPOKESMAN B: Perhaps you could make a better line.

SPOKESMAN A: We're all listening. What have you got against this line?

A1: Chickens.

As AND Bs: Chickens? What have chickens got to do with it? Take no notice. Got chickens on the brain.

A1: I know something about chickens, I do. There's not much you can tell me about chickens. I was brought up with chickens. And I'll tell you this: chickens can't read.

SPOKESMAN B: Chickens can't read?

SPOKESMAN A: What difference does that make to this line?

A1:   None at all to your line.

SPOKESMAN B: Or to your chickens for that matter.

A1:   No use putting up your 'Beware of the Bull' signs. No use sticking up your 'Trespassers will be Prosecuted'* notices. And you might as well forget your 'One-Way Streets', your 'Diversions', and your 'Roads Closed'. The chickens go where they want to go. No use drawing a line, and expecting the chickens to stay on this side of it. Or on that side of it for that matter.

As AND Bs: True. That's a point. I never saw a chicken reading. Or taking any notice of a line.

SPOKESMAN B: But what does it matter where the chickens go?

A1:   Oh, if it doesn't matter there's no more to be said.

SPOKESMAN A: Good. Now we can get on with . . .

A2:   But suppose it should be sheep.

B1:   Sheep?

A2:   Sheep can't read either. At least I never saw a sheep reading. Ignorant animals really.

B1:   A line won't keep a sheep from straying.

B2:   Especially if they can't read.

A3:   Or cows from wandering.

B3:   Or horses from getting lost.

A2:   And as for rabbits . . .

SPOKESMAN B: All right. What do you want?

SPOKESMAN A: Schools for animals?

A1:   What we need are fences.

B1:   Walls.

A2:   Thick enough to stop cows from breaking through.

B2:   High enough to stop chickens from flying over.

A3:   Good walls make good neighbours.

B3:   Good neighbours make good walls.

SPOKESMAN A: You want walls?

SPOKESMAN B: Shall we build walls?

A1:   Before we do anything else.

> SPOKESMAN A *and* SPOKESMAN B *take opposite ends of the piece of string, and raise it about six inches off the ground.*

SPOKESMAN A: This high?

B1:   Higher. Think of the cows.

The string is raised waist high.

SPOKESMAN B: This high?
A2:   Higher. Think of the horses.

The string is raised shoulder high.

SPOKESMAN A: This high?
B2:   Higher. Think of the chickens.

> *The string is held as high as the* SPOKESMEN *can reach, standing on tiptoe.*

SPOKESMAN B: I think that should do.
B1:   Yes, that should do.
SPOKESMAN A: It had better do. Now make it fast.

The ends of the string are tied to posts.

SPOKESMAN B: And build the wall.

> *The wall is built. This can be done in a number of ways. Blocks could be built up to the height of the string, or more string could be tied between the posts, or material could be draped over the string. At all events it is achieved after a great deal of activity. Meanwhile, the* RECORDER *looks on, and takes notes.*

RECORDER: I won't say they're right. I won't say they're wrong. It's my job merely to record events. Events speak for themselves. They wanted a wall: they've got a wall. Neither side can see over, or through, or round. That's a wall.

> *Now all the As are on one side of the wall, and all the Bs are on the other side.*

SPOKESMAN A: That's a wall. That ought to last.
SPOKESMAN B: Nothing we need to learn about making a wall.
RECORDER: Except how to make a way over, or through, or round.
SPOKESMAN A: Are you there?
SPOKESMAN B: We're here. Are you all satisfied?
SPOKESMAN A: Everything went according to plan. What now?
SPOKESMAN B: We settle down.* And you?
SPOKESMAN A: We settle down, too. It's good land.

SPOKESMAN B: It's very good land. We're lucky. We've got good neighbours.

SPOKESMAN A: We've got good neighbours, too. It's a good wall.

SPOKESMAN B: Good walls make good neighbours.

SPOKESMAN A: Good neighbours make good walls.

SPOKESMAN B: Good-bye, then. There's work to be done.

SPOKESMAN A: Good-bye. Must get down to work.

Shouting 'Good-bye' the two groups pick up their belongings, and move away. The 'Good-byes' die away in the distance.

RECORDER: Nothing left but the wall. And the chickens on each side of the wall. And the sheep on each side of the wall. And the cows on each side of the wall. And the horses on each side of the wall. And the people on each side of the wall . . .

The groups re-appear on each side of the wall. They are all working.

It's a busy life — and the great advantage with being busy is that it occupies the mind. Working keeps thoughts under control. Thoughts are more apt to* run wild than any sheep. Thoughts can fly higher than any chickens. In fact walls make thoughts fly even higher. But as long as thoughts are kept under control there's no harm done. Except that there comes a time when all the chickens have been fed; all the cows have been milked; all the sheep have been rounded up in the fold* — and thoughts are free to stray.

Gradually the groups give up work, and make themselves comfortable.

A1: I wonder what they're doing over there.

A2: Over there?

B1: Over there. What do you think they're doing?

A2: Why?

A1: Why not?

A2: Why do you wonder what they're doing over there?

B1: We can't see them, can we?

B2: They can't see us.

A1: I just wondered.

B1: Anybody can wonder.

A1: Just a thought — like do spring and summer come before autumn and winter, or do autumn and winter come first?

B1: Like — can a worm think?

A1: Like — what are they doing over there?

A2: The usual things, I suppose.

B2: They'll be doing the usual things.

A1: What do you mean — the usual things?

A2: Things that you usually do.

B2: Things that we usually do.

B1: Not the things that *they* usually do?

A2: The things that they usually do.

B1: You said the things that *we* usually do.

A2: They're the same things.

B1: Are they the same?

A2: Why shouldn't they be the same?

B2: Why should they be the same?

A1: They're not like us.

A2: Aren't they?

B1: It stands to reason.*

A1: Work it out for yourself.*

B1: Just work it out.

A1: For instance — you're not like me, are you?

A2: Not much.

B1: You're not a bit like me.

A2: So they're not like us.

B2: So they're not a bit like us.

A2: We're on this side of the wall.

B2: They're on the other side of the wall.

A1: Fancy* living on the other side of the wall.

B1: Fancy wanting to live on the other side of the wall.

A2: When you could be living here.

B2: Fancy not wanting to live here.

A1: Funny.

B1: They've got some funny ways.

A1: Yes, they've got some funny ways.

B2: Have they?

A2: Of course. You've got some funny ways, too.

B1: They look funny to me all right.

A2: We've all got funny ways.

B2: But their ways are funnier. Over there.

B1: We don't even know what ways they've got.

A2:   If they've got ways we don't know about, they must be funny ways.

A1:   Still, as long as they're on the other side of the wall, it doesn't matter.

B1:   It doesn't matter as long as they're on that side, and we're on this.

A2:   I'm not so sure.

A1:   What do you mean?

B1:   I've been thinking. They're very quiet.

B2:   We're quiet.

B1:   We've got nothing to make a noise about.

A2:   What about them, eh?

A1:   What about them?

A2:   What have they got to be so quiet about?

B1:   It's unnatural.

A1:   It's unusual.

B2:   It's disturbing.

A2:   It's disquieting.*

B1:   It's abnormal.

A1:   It's uncomfortable.

B2:   It's sinister.*

A2:   It's not as it should be.

B1:   It's enough to send cold shivers* down your back.

A1:   It's enough to make your hair stand on end.

B2:   Just thinking about it.

A2:   Just wondering.

B1:   What are they up to?

A2:   What are they doing behind that wall?

B2:   They could be doing anything behind that wall.

B1:   Like what?

A2:   Just think.

B1:   Ah!

B2:   Oh!

A1:   They wouldn't.

B2:   Not that!

A2:   I wouldn't put it past 'em.*

B2:   Not them!

A1:   Not that!

A2:   Not what?

A1:   Not what you're thinking.

B2:   Oh, would they really?

B1:   They're not to be relied on.

A1:   You're exaggerating.

A2:   Exaggerating?

A1:   You wouldn't expect anybody to do that.

B2:   We wouldn't do it.

B1:   We're not like them.

A2:   They're not like us.

B2:   But they wouldn't. Not . . .

B1:   Like . . .

A2:   For instance . . .

B1:   Or even . . .

A1:   Not to mention . . .

A2:   Just you wait.

A1:   Wait for what?

B1:   You'll see. You'll believe me then.

A2:   Just you wait till you see it happening.

B2:   I don't believe it.

A1:   Oh!

A2:   You will.

B1:   If you ask me, they're wicked.

B2:   Stands to reason. They're a wicked lot.

A1:   They wouldn't get up to that sort of thing if they weren't
      wicked.

A2:   Well, as long as they're wicked on their side of the wall . . .

A1:   Wickedness spreads.

B1:   Wickedness creeps.

A2:   How long will they go on being wicked on their side of the
      wall?

B2:   It's a high wall.

A1:   It's a thick wall.

B3:   Let them do what they like on their side of the wall.

A3:   They can't interfere with us.

A1:   Can't they?

B1:   What can they do to us?

A2:   They could be making plans now.

B2:   Think. Just think.

A1:   They could be spying on us now.

B3:   Don't be silly.

A3:   That's absurd.

A1:   Is it?

B1: Perhaps we ought to check.
A2: It wouldn't do any harm to look.
A3: You can look if you like.
B3: I'm not making a fool of myself.
A3: I'll tell you what they're doing on the other side.
A2: What?
B3: I know what they're doing.
B2: Tell us.
A3: They're lying down in the sun like sensible people, maybe chewing long bits of grass.
B3: They're looking up at the sky, and working out tomorrow's weather.
A3: Or they're counting chickens.
B3: Or counting sheep.
A3: They're doing what we're doing.
B3: They're doing exactly what we're doing.
A1: I knew they weren't to be trusted.
B1: Have a look quickly.
A2: Look at them.
B2: Look.
A1: Look.
B1: How?
A2: Climb up.
B2: Look over the top.

> *They prepare to climb the wall with whatever means are at hand — blocks, furniture, or each other.*

RECORDER: At this point there is always the temptation to shout 'stop'. But a Recorder mustn't. It's a Recorder's job to record: no more, no less. And, my goodness the fuss that's made about handwriting and spelling! As if spelling mattered after ... they've taken the first steps, you see. And after the first steps the others follow naturally. All a Recorder can do is to record. They climb to the top of the wall, and ...

> *The As, who have now reached the top of the wall, come face to face with the Bs. They all shriek, and clamber down again.*

A1: It's all true.
B1: They were.
A1: Looking over.

B1:   Spying.

A1:   On us.

B1:   On us.

A1:   It's a good job we looked.

B1:   We caught them at it.

A1:   And were they surprised!

B1:   They never expected that.

A1:   They were fairly caught.

B1:   Caught in the act.

A2:   But why were they doing it?

B2:   Why would they want to do it?

A2:   Why?

B2:   Why?

A1:   Ah-ha.

B1:   We can guess.

A1:   That's only half the story.

B1:   That's only the tip of the iceberg.*

A1:   They're up to no good.

B1:   They're ready for something.

A1:   We must be ready for them.

B2:   Ready for what?

A1:   Ready for anything.

B1:   Anything might happen.

A1:   They're not like us.

B1:   They're a bad lot.

A1:   They're cruel.

B1:   They're ruthless.*

A1:   Devilish.

B1:   Fiendish.*

A1:   Wild.

B1:   Savages.

A1:   Peeping Toms.*

B1:   Sneaks.*

A3:   But let's consider.

B3:   Let's think carefully.

A3:   We looked over the wall, too.

B3:   We'd never have seen them if we hadn't peeped.

A1:   It's as well that we did.

B1:   Where should we be now if we hadn't?

A3:   Wait, though. Couldn't we forget that it happened?

B3:   Couldn't we make allowances?

A1: Oh, yes, indeed.

B1: Why not, indeed?

A1: If we *want* to be made into mince.*

B1: If we want to wake up with our throats cut.

A2: But what can we do?

B2: What's to be done?

A1: One thing's certain.

B1: There's no doubt at all.

A1: We can't live here any longer with them just there.

B1: We'll either have to fight or move on.

A1: Either they go, or we'll have to go.

B1: It's them or us.

As AND Bs: Them.

A3: But we've got the wall.

B3: There's always the wall.

As AND Bs: Pull it down. Pull it down.

Both sides attack the wall.

RECORDER: It's odd: even sensible actions that would never be taken in the cause of peace are taken in the name of war. Like all pulling together. Like breaking down walls. But the result isn't the same. As for instance . . .

The wall falls. For a second the two sides stare at each other. Then, with a cry, they rush at each other. They fight.

Some are forced off-stage. Some run off-stage and are pursued. Some fall and are dragged away by friends.

They fight. No, I'm not recording all the details. Any battle is just like any other battle. There are some acts of chivalry,* some deeds of treachery,* a hint of courage, a touch of cowardice. But the heroes, and the cowards, and the patriots, and the traitors have one thing in common: they all end up as dead as each other. This is nothing. I've seen battles that make this look like a squabble between stickle-backs.* Not that I'm offering any prizes for the best battle. Every battle ends in the same way. One side thinks it has won; the other side thinks it ought to have won. Someone cleans up the mess, and the ground is left clean and tidy — ready for someone else to fight over another time. I could moralize.* I could draw conclusions. But the conclusion is so

obvious. The facts speak for themselves. They fight until . . .
Oh, is it over already?

The stage is clear.

Now, is there anything to add before I draw the line?* No? I
had a feeling that there might be. Like the last spark in a
dying fire. Like the last syllable of a fading echo. Ah, I
thought as much.

*An A and a B limp on to the stage from opposite sides. They
come face to face where the wall once stood.*

A: Going?

B: Going.

A: You could stay — now.

B: No, we can't stay — now.

A: It's good land.

B: It was good land.

A: We — we didn't want to — to . . .

B: If only we hadn't . . .

A: But you . . .

B: We?

A: We, too.

B: It was the wall, you know.

A: The wall was to blame.

B: The wall.

A: The wall.

B: We should have made it stronger.

A: Thicker.

B: Higher.

A: Longer.

B: It was the wall.

They go out on opposite sides.

The RECORDER *slams the book shut, and jumps up angrily.*

RECORDER: I don't want to know any more. It's all down here.
Over and over again. History. The record is kept because
someday someone may learn from it. Now I'm required
elsewhere. Oh, this all becomes so monotonous.* (*He starts
to walk away, but pauses*) Someday. Somewhere. Someone.
Is it possible? Hah!

He goes. BLACKOUT.

Glossary

The meanings given below are those which the words and phrases have as they occur in the play.

Page
71   *Worn out*: very tired.
     ponders: thinks.
     taken with: interested in.
72   *tramped*: walked over long distances.
     mean: average.
     lush pasturage: thickly-growing grassland.
     goes into a huddle: crowds closely together.
     warily: cautiously, suspecting danger.
73   *negotiations*: discussions in order to reach an agreement on something.
     Proposals etc.: all the many bureaucratic arrangements made in order to reach a democratic political decision.
     natural amenities: natural advantages and resources.
     grazing rights: a person's right to let his/her cattle feed (graze) in a particular place.
74   *musing*: thinking to himself.
     Good fences make good neighbours: a well-known quotation from "Mending Wall", a poem by the American poet, Robert Frost.
     pegging out: marking out lines on the ground.
75   *'Trespassers will be Prosecuted'*: a sign that shows it is illegal to walk on a certain piece of land.
76   *settle down*: start living in a regular way.
77   *apt to*: likely to.
     rounded up in the fold: collected together behind fences.
78   *It stands to reason*: it is obvious.
     Work it out for yourself: come to your own conclusions.
     Fancy: imagine.
79   *disquieting*: makes one feel uneasy.
     sinister: evil.
     shivers: the shaking caused by fear.
     I wouldn't put it past 'em (coll.): it is possible they would do that (something bad).
82   *tip of the iceberg*: a small part of the whole truth.
     ruthless: without pity, cruel.
     Fiendish: devilish, cruel.
     Peeping Toms: people who spy on others when they think they are alone.
     Sneaks: cowards, people who tell stories about others.

83   *made into mince*:   cut to pieces.
     chivalry: honourable, courageous behaviour.
     treachery: falseness.
     a squabble between sticklebacks: a very small and
     unimportant fight (a stickleback is a small fish).
     moralize: say what is right and wrong.
84   *draw the line*:   finish the story.
     monotonous: uninteresting because it repeats itself.

Questions

> OUTLINE TO QUESTIONS
>
> 1.   characterization: the Recorder
> 2.   characterization: group A, group B
> 3. and 4.   theme

1. What role does the Recorder play in *Us and Them*?

    (a) What details in the Recorder's opening speech show that
         the action that is about to take place has happened
         before (p. 71)?
    (b) What sort of thing does he record (p. 71)?
    (c) What good does he hope it will do (pp. 83−84)? Is he
         optimistic?
    (d) How enthusiastic is the Recorder about 'Democracy'?
         What form does 'Democracy' take in *Us and Them*
         (p. 73)?
    (e) Look at these lines, spoken by the Recorder, in their
         context, and decide in what tone of voice they should be
         said (e.g. ironic, calm and cool, sad, angry etc.):
            'The record has to be kept. Who knows − one day
            someone may learn from it.' (p. 74)
            '. . . the heroes, and the cowards, and the patriots, and
            the traitors have one thing in common: they all end up
            as dead as each other.' (p. 83)
            'I don't want to know any more. It's all down here.
            Over and over again. History.' (p. 84)
    (f) The Recorder *'jumps up angrily'* to say the last speech.
         Has he been angry before? Do you think the last speech
         would be more effective if it were said calmly (p. 84)?

2. The Recorder says 'Thoughts are more apt to run wild than any sheep.' (p. 77). How does the dialogue between the building of the wall (p. 76) and looking over the wall (p. 81) show the development of these thoughts?

   (a) After the wall is built, the two groups start thinking what the others are doing. Is either group worried about the other at this point? Consider, for example:
   > B1: '... What do you think they're doing? (p. 77)
   > A1: Just a thought — like do spring and summer come before autumn and winter ...' (p. 78)

   (b) At what point do you think the groups start to get worried?

   (c) If you were directing the play, would you have the groups acting most worried and panic-stricken just before they look over the wall (p. 81) or at an earlier point? If earlier, where?

   (d) Look at these lines in their contexts, and decide in what tone of voice they should be said (e.g. self-satisfied, confident, worried, puzzled etc.):
   > B2: '... they're not a bit like us.' (p. 78)
   > A1: 'Fancy living on the other side of the wall.' (p. 78)
   > B1: 'They've got some funny ways.' (p. 79)
   > A1: 'It's enough to make your hair stand on end.' (p. 79)
   > A2: 'How long will they go on being wicked on their side of the wall?' (p. 80)
   > A1: 'I knew they weren't to be trusted.' (p. 81)

   (e) Write down what you think A1, A2, B1 and B2 are thinking by completing their interrupted sentences (p. 80):
   > B2: 'But they wouldn't. Not ...
   > B1: Like ...
   > A2: For instance ...
   > B1: Or even ...
   > A1: Not to mention ...'

   Why has the playwright not completed their thoughts?

   (f) Look at the dialogue from B3: 'Let them do what they like on their side of the wall.' (p. 80) to B2: 'Look over the top.' (p. 81) Do all the characters act in the same way, or do some seem to have more common sense?

3. Why and in what ways does Campton show human actions to be childish?

   (a) 'Good fences/walls make good neighbours. Good neighbours make good fences/walls.' (p. 74, p. 75, p. 77) is repeated more than once. Why do the two parties enjoy repeating these phrases?

(b) There is much repetition about the way different animals could climb over the walls (pp. 75–76). What sort of story books frequently involve repetition and tales about animals?

(c) If you were directing the play, would you have the Recorder appear much older than the members of the two parties? Why/why not?

(d) After the battle, is there any point at which the two parties admit their own guilt? Where (p. 84)?

(e) Has anything been learnt from the battle? Why/why not (p. 84)?

4. In the production note (p. 70) Campton writes '. . . there is no difference between the people on either side of the wall. They are really part of one group.' How does Campton suggest that differences and difficulties are of our own making?

(a) Consider the title of the play. Who in the play are 'Us' and who 'Them'? Does the title suggest that people are united or divided?

(b) When the two groups arrive (p. 71) they say almost the same things:

   A1:   'This is our place.
   B1:   Ours.'

And later:

   B3:   'They're doing exactly what we're doing.
   A1:   I knew they weren't to be trusted.' (p. 81)

What is ironic about these two pieces of dialogue?

(c) Why is it that both groups find the 'good place' but only notice each other later (pp. 71–72)?

(d) What does the Recorder say about sensible actions being taken in time of war that might more appropriately be taken in time of peace (p. 83)?

(e) Why do you think one of the first stage directions is '*Parties A and B enter from opposite sides.*' (p. 71) and one of the last is '*They go out on opposite sides.*' (p. 84)?

Drama Activities

Choose *ONE* of these situations. Prepare a sketch in pairs and practise it within your own group. It may then be shown to the whole group.

1. Two people are shipwrecked on a desert island. They may know each other (friends, husband and wife, manager and assistant etc.) or they may never have met before. They begin in a friendly way but soon irritations and then suspicions creep in.

    Possible development

    —   Irritation at the way the other eats/doesn't wash enough/doesn't do a fair share of work etc.
    —   Suspicion that the other may be planning to escape alone/keeping a secret supply of food/planning to murder you etc.

    > USEFUL COLLOQUIAL EXPRESSIONS
    >
    > *Irritation*
    >
    > I can't stand the way you ...
    > I can't stand it when you ...
    > It really gets on my nerves when you ...
    > It drives me mad/up the wall when you ...
    >
    > *Suspicion*
    >
    > I wouldn't put it past you to ...
    > I don't know what you'd get up to if I didn't ...
    > You could be ... for all I know.
    > If I didn't know better I'd say you were ...

2. Two people (friends, a couple, work partners etc.) are eating at a restaurant. Conversation soon comes to a stop. The dialogue then becomes the unspoken thoughts of each person.

    Possible development

    —   Worry about what the other person is thinking/worry about appearance, clothes etc./thoughts about the things you dislike in the other (see *irritation* above) or suspect the other person of (see *suspicion* above).

    Bring your dialogue to a conclusion (either by starting to talk to each other again, or by leaving each other in silence).

3. A couple discuss the new neighbours who have just moved in next door. It is clear that the couple do not like them and are suspicious of them (see *Useful colloquial expressions* above).

Staging

How many characters would you have? Would you have an equal number of male and female actors?

Should the Recorder keep to one place or move around during the action?

What is happening to the other characters when the Recorder is speaking?

Should the Recorder be lit by spotlight for his speeches?

What props would you use (see Campton's suggestions for constructing a wall, p. 76)?

How comic or serious, stylised or realistic would you make the battle scenes?

*   *   *   *   *

Over The Wall and Us And Them: comparative questions

1. Compare the Narrator and the Recorder in the two plays. Why is one called a Narrator and the other a Recorder? Is one more involved in the dramatic action taking place than the other, or are they both detached and ironic? Look at the final speeches of the Narrator and the Recorder. Are both plays equally pessimistic?

2. Clichés and mottos appear in both plays (see, for example, phrases of *Acceptance*, p. 67 or question 3(a), p 87. Do you have similar expressions in your own language? Does one play use more clichés than the other? What points are the playwrights making about why people use language in this way?

3. Neither play has characters in the conventional sense. What has been gained from this? Which play seems to you more successful in projecting character onto the numbered speeches? Do you think both playwrights are equally concerned with characterization?

4. Does one play have a more serious message than the other? Did you find one play funnier than the other? Are both plays making serious points through comedy? Which play did you find more satisfying?

RELATIONSHIPS
(Comedies)

Lyndon Brook

Lyndon Brook was born in America in 1926, and has lived in Britain since 1942. He is both an actor and a playwright. His plays include two historical dramas, *Fool's Mate* (1953) and *Rogue Prince* (1958), and two thrillers, *Love Her to Death!* (1955) and *The Uninvited Host* (1964). *Score* is taken from *Mixed Doubles* (1970), an entertainment on marriage, which also includes one-act plays by James Saunders, David Campton and Harold Pinter.

THE PLAY

Harry and Sheila are playing tennis and trying very hard to be a match for their successful and attractive opponents, Jim and Jane.

CHARACTERS

HARRY
SHEILA

SCORE

A tennis net is stretched across stage over the floats. *
HARRY *and* SHEILA, *in white, hold rackets, but mime the use
of tennis balls.*

HARRY (*not pleased*): That's another game* to you two . . .
(*Lifts his head at some remark from our side of the net.*) Now
Jim! Don't you start feeling sorry for us — this is all part of
our tactics, we're lulling* you into a false sense of
superiority!

SHEILA (*collecting balls upstage*): False?

HARRY (*to query from* JANE): Score? Ah yes . . . (*Clicking his
fingers at* SHEILA) Sheila, what's the score?

SHEILA: Don't you click your fingers at me! We're losing. I can
tell that much.

HARRY: Very helpful.

SHEILA: Well, for heaven's sake, you're supposed to be keeping
it!

HARRY: Let's see . . . it's your serve . . .

SHEILA: I know we've won two games . . .

HARRY: And I started serving this set* . . .

SHEILA: I *think* it's two — five. (*She indicates her side and
opponents' side of net.*)

HARRY: Hell, really? (*Turns front.*) Know the score, Jim? . . .
Two — *four*! . . . No, no. (*Pleased*) If you say so — we've — er
— we've lost count! (*Traps ball from* JIM.) Thanks! (*Traps
ball from* JANE *right.*) Grazie* (*pronounced Grahtsy-eh*)
Jane! Sheila's serve! (*Throws ball back in general direction
of* SHEILA.) Put it on his backhand.* (*Settles and smiles at*
JANE.)

Slight pause. SHEILA *is getting her hair in place, then
collects two balls and comes to base line* * *to serve.*

(*To* JANE) Sorry, was I staring? . . . Oh! Your hair! I thought
you said my . . . I think it looks wonderful . . . I wish you'd
tell Sheila where you go: she has such a terrible time

keeping it even presentable!* . . . Oh yes, the hair's all right
— it's what she does with it, poor darling.

SHEILA *serves.* HARRY *misses* JIM'S *return.*

Damn! Good shot, Jim! (*To* JANE) Better keep my eye on
the *ball*! (*To* SHEILA) I said his *back*hand!

SHEILA   (*calm*): It was the wind.

HARRY: Oh. (*Then, realising*) There's not a *breath* of wind!

*He has crossed down right.** SHEILA *collects balls on way up
left.*

SHEILA: Love — fifteen.*

SHEILA *serves. Into the net.* HARRY *picks it up quickly. On*
SHEILA'S *second serve* HARRY *misses* JANE'S *sideline**
return.

(*Sweetly*) Wouldn't you be more use back here, darling?

HARRY: Server's partner always stands at the net.

SHEILA: Only when he can make contact with the occasional
ball, surely.

SHEILA *goes right to pick up ball.* HARRY *crosses down left
and talks across right to* JANE.

HARRY: Afraid we're not giving you much of a match,* Jane . . .
Oh, well, if you play every week! . . . No, Sheila always seems
to have so much to do — in the house . . . Oh yes, au-pairs* —
they never stay, though.

SHEILA: Love — thirty.*

HARRY: We've a Belgian girl at the moment . . .

SHEILA: You'll get hurt, Harry, if you stand so far over as that!

HARRY   (*moving left but continuing talking to* JANE): But I
caught *her* looking up the cross-Channel ferries* yesterday.

SHEILA *serves. Into the net.* HARRY *picks up the ball.*

Sheila just can't get on with them.

SHEILA *serves again. Into net.* HARRY *picks it up.*

Double.*

SHEILA   (*cutting but smiling*): Yes, I saw.

HARRY   (*to* JANE):   *I* find them — stimulating. They keep you
young!

SHEILA: Balls;* please. (*She is up left.*)

> HARRY *bounces the two balls he has in his hand back to her.*

> Love — forty.*

> SHEILA *serves.* HARRY *takes vicious swipe* at the return and wins the point.*

HARRY: Grazie, Jim, it wasn't too bad, was it!
SHEILA: Fifteen — forty.

> HARRY *hasn't moved.*

> (*Repeats*) Fifteen — forty. (*Pause.*) Other side,* Harry.

HARRY: Oh, (*Moves left speaks right to* JANE) That's my best shot — I've been trying to get it back all day!

> SHEILA *serves. It hits* HARRY *on the neck.*

> Ow!

SHEILA: I warned you — you were practically on the centre line!*

HARRY (*to* JANE): I suppose that's what they call a lethal* serve.

> HARRY *moves further left.* SHEILA *serves. The return goes to her and she drives to* JANE. HARRY *repeats his swipe and wins the point.*

> That's better! (*Crossing right.*) *Thirty* — forty! Now, we need a couple more like that . . .

SHEILA: *I* need something to serve with.
HARRY: Eh? Oh . . . (*Starts looking for balls.*)
SHEILA (*trapping one and then another from* JIM): Thank you, Jim. (*Low*) Glad someone has some manners.
HARRY: Oh, stop nagging.*
SHEILA: Thirty — forty, then.

> *She serves from up left.* HARRY *takes third swipe, grins delightedly at the result and starts to turn upstage.* *

HARRY: Deuce!* (*Stops centre and turns to* JIM.) *Out*?! (*Looks at* SHEILA.) Out?! (*Then back at* JIM.) Are you sure, Jim? . . . No, no, I just thought . . . Oh, thanks, Jane, no, there's no need to play it again — if *you* say . . . (*Slight pause.*) I must admit I thought . . .
SHEILA: Don't argue, Harry.

HARRY *moves back towards* SHEILA.

SHEILA: Your game, then ... (*She hits ball across to* JANE. *Turns to* HARRY.) Five — two.

HARRY: Did it look out to you?

SHEILA: Couldn't possibly tell from back here. I take Jim's word.

HARRY: You would. (*Throws a couple of balls over net from baseline.*) Your serve, Jane.

SHEILA: Don't know what's worrying you. Thought you wanted them to win.

HARRY: What on earth are you talking about?

SHEILA: You said it might make things easier at the office ...

HARRY: If we didn't beat them by too wide a margin,* you idiot! I never said ...

SHEILA: Well, that's not very likely, is it, the way you're playing!

HARRY: And you're Virginia Wade,* I suppose! If you're so ...

SHEILA: What were you nattering to Jane about?

HARRY: Oh, this and that ... What Jim? Oh yes, we're ready.

SHEILA: You'd do better to concentrate on the game. Tennis.

HARRY (*to* JIM): Just a little conference on tactics. (*Moves to net left.*) Yes, Jane: five — two ... Cinque — due* (*Cheenkweh—Dooeh.*)

SHEILA (*mutters*): Eight days in San Remo* ...

SHEILA *receives serve. Her return is smashed by* JIM.

HARRY: Shot, Jim! (*To* SHEILA) You gave it to him on a plate!*

SHEILA: Couldn't help it — my racket slipped.

HARRY: That's just your trouble — you don't use the right grip. Your racket can't slip if you hold it properly: like this. (*He demonstrates.*) Look — *you* hold it like *this*!

SHEILA: Who's nagging now? ... Here you are, Jane! (*Throws ball across and moves down right to net position and talks across to* JIM *left.*) What, Jim? ... Oh, do you think so? (*Looks down at, smoothes her dress.*) How nice of you to say ... Heavens no, I made it myself, from a pattern ... I'm lucky to be able to buy darning wool* on the dress allowance* Harry gives me ... I'm always green with envy at Jane's clothes.

HARRY *receives* JANE'S *serve. His return is smashed by* JIM.

SHEILA: What was that about handing it on a plate?

HARRY: It was Jane's serve. It was a brute! . . . Lovely serve, Janey!

SHEILA: Janey? Since when Janey?

HARRY: Everyone calls her that.

SHEILA: I don't.

HARRY: Come on . . . it's thirty — love.

SHEILA, *up right, returns* JANE'S *serve.*

Well done.

HARRY, *at net left, returns next shot,* SHEILA *the next, but when ball comes back fourth time* HARRY *makes attempt to stretch across right.*

All right, mine! (*Misses it.*) No — yours!

But SHEILA *has changed courts by now and can't retrieve* * HARRY'S *miss.*

SHEILA: Oh charming! I could have got it perfectly well if you . . .

HARRY   (*becoming more and more tense*): Then why didn't you!

He picks up two balls at baseline and smashes them across net. SHEILA *walks to position at net right.*

SHEILA: Calm down, darling, it's only a game. (*To* JIM) Honestly, I don't know what's the matter with Harry today — he's right off* . . . Yes, he should, you're right . . . It's all I can do to get him out to post a letter sometimes . . . He comes back from the office and just slumps* in a chair watching television . . . (*Laughs.*) Oh yes, he always watches Wimbledon* . . . you'd never have guessed it, would you!

HARRY: Sheila! It's forty — love! Match point!*

SHEILA: Well, try not to send this one straight to Jimmy . . . (*Smiles at* JIM.) He's got a terrific smash.

HARRY: Got a terrific what?

SHEILA   (*dry and clipped*):   Smash.

HARRY *returns* JANE'S *serve to* JANE. *Ball comes back to* SHEILA *who plays it to* JIM. JIM *smashes to* HARRY *who, wide left, gets it back to* JANE. JANE'S *shot comes back very high and* SHEILA *starts to run backwards.*

All right!

HARRY: *I* can!

He hopping sideways from left, she hopping backwards from right, eyes on the high ball, bump and land on their knees. Then the ball lands on HARRY'S *head.*

Typical! Is there nothing you can do right?!

SHEILA: Oh, Harry — for God's sake . . .

HARRY: I had a chance at a beautiful shot, so of course I get knocked out of the way. Hell, Sheila, it's not as if you were good at anything else — it's the same casual, half-hearted, sloppy* approach to everything that makes you such a mess as a person!

SHEILA: My approach . . .

HARRY: It's only a game! Isn't that what you said? Only a game! So that means you don't have to put anything into it — just slop along and titter* when you make a complete fool of yourself — and me — (*Turning still full of anger.*) Yes Jim, what is it?!

SHEILA: He said it's only a game.

Pause while HARRY *looks at each of them, calms himself, and musters a smile.*

HARRY: Well, I suppose we should be thankful there are no bones broken! Well! Game, set and match! (*Approaches net.*) Well played you two!

SHEILA: Beaten fair and square.

HARRY (*to* JANE): Mmm? . . . No, no — please go on, Jane — I'm always glad to learn from an expert . . . How do you mean, my grip? . . . Oh yes? . . . Well . . . I must try to remember that (*Trying it.*) Yes . . . see that, darling?

SHEILA (*mild*): Yes.

HARRY: Thank you, Jane . . .

SHEILA (*to* JIM): No, we're in no hurry, are we, Harry.

HARRY: No . . . Lovely! But I insist on buying them* . . . No, Jim, I insist! . . . No. I'm not going to have you buying . . .

SHEILA (*interrupts*): Well, the *second* round,* then. Come on, Harry, help me collect the balls.

HARRY (*to* JIM *and* JANE): No, you go ahead — we'll be right with you.

HARRY *moves to help* SHEILA. *They both stop and look after their departing opponents.*

(*Sighing*):   I suppose we need more practice.

SHEILA: Intensive training, if you're hoping tennis will help your career.

HARRY: Sorry, darling.

SHEILA: It's all right. There are some behind you. (*He leaves her.*) If only you didn't get so het up!*

HARRY: Maybe I should take up bridge — not half as exhausting.

SHEILA: You'd be that much closer to Janey at the card table.

HARRY: You *jealous*?

SHEILA: Oh, now, Harry, darling, please. Even you can't seriously think you'd get anywhere with *that* one. How could I possibly be jealous?

HARRY: Oh.

SHEILA: Besides, you can tell they're both mad about each other.*

HARRY: Yes . . . I must admit, I see Jim's point! She's quite a girl.

SHEILA: Oh, I never denied that — they're a very handsome couple.

HARRY (*thinking of* JANE):   Beautiful.

SHEILA: The trouble is, they *know* it. (*Points.*) There's one over there. And all the time she must spend — to say nothing of money — keeping up that glossy look* . . . lovely, I know — but is it *worth* it!

HARRY: I imagine Jim thinks so. Of course, he's the brainy one of the two — brilliant at the office, you know. I really wasn't jealous when he was promoted — he deserved it.

SHEILA: He always gives me the feeling of pressure . . . that his brain's ticking away . . .

HARRY: Yes . . . Well, let's face it, you can be too clever, can't you. I mean . . . it's brought him a good job and wonderful prospects* — but the strain of always keeping one jump ahead — trying to outguess everyone else — I don't think I could live like that.

SHEILA: No . . .

HARRY: That the lot?

SHEILA (*She glances into the box he holds.*):   Six. Yes.

HARRY: Come along then, Miss Wade . . .

SHEILA: Yes, Mr Laver* — or may I call you 'Rod'?

They move downstage to follow JIM *and* JANE.

HARRY (*Stops.*): Yes ... they may be attractive, and clever, successful, well-adjusted ... and happy ... but don't let's fool ourselves, there's more to life than that, isn't there.

SHEILA *turns to look at him as BLACKOUT.*

Glossary

The meanings given below are those which the words and phrases have as they occur in the play.

Page
93   *floats*:   footlights, the lights at the front of the stage which shine on the actors.

game: unit in a set (see below), in which, in order to win, the player(s) must score at least four points and be two points ahead of the opponent(s).

lulling: calming by deceptive means.

set: unit of a match in tennis, in which one player or pair of players must win at least six games.

Grazie (Italian):   thank you.

backhand: a way of hitting a tennis ball by holding the racket across his body to make the shot.

base line: the back line of a tennis court.

94   *presentable*:   fit to be seen in public.

He has crossed down right: after each point, the serving side move either right or left.

Love—fifteen: 'love' means zero; 'fifteen' means that Jim and Jane have won the first point.

sideline: line that marks the side boundary of the tennis court.

match: contest.

au-pairs: young foreign girls who live with British families in return for doing light household jobs.

Love—thirty: the second point has gone to Jim and Jane.

cross-Channel ferries: boats that go between England and the European mainland.

Double: two serving faults (giving a point to the opposition).

95   *Balls*:   both 'May I have some balls?' and a taboo slang word meaning nonsense.

Love—forty: the third point has gone to Jim and Jane.

vicious swipe: sweeping blow, aggressively struck.

Other side: Harry has not yet moved to the other side of the court as he should do.

centre line: the line in the middle of the tennis court.

lethal: deadly, very effective.

nagging: continuously complaining.

upstage: the back of the stage.

Deuce: forty—forty, three points each.

96   *margin*:   amount.

Virginia Wade: one of the best-known British women tennis players.

Cinque—due (Italian): five—two.

San Remo: an Italian holiday resort popular with British tourists.

gave it to him on a plate: made it too easy for him.

darning wool: wool used for repairing clothes.

dress allowance: money given for buying clothes.

97   *retrieve*: return successfully.

right off: not at his best at all.

slumps: falls heavily.

Wimbledon: famous international tennis championship held in South London.

Match point: final point needed by the leading players to win the competition.

98   *sloppy*: careless.

titter: laugh in a silly way, trying to hide the laughter.

them: the drinks.

round: number of drinks bought at one time for a group of people.

99   *het up*: excited, nervy.

mad about each other: very much in love.

glossy look: attractive and stylish appearance.

prospects: chances of success in his job.

Mr Laver: Rod Laver, a well-known Australian tennis champion.

Questions

> OUTLINE TO QUESTIONS
>
> 1—3.   characterization: Harry and Sheila
> 4.   theme/characterization: Harry and Sheila

1. What sort of relationship do Harry and Sheila have?

    (a) Why does Harry use Italian phrases from time to time (p. 93, p. 95, p. 96)?

    (b) What does Sheila think of this (p. 96)?

    (c) Is it only Sheila's tennis playing that Harry finds irritating about her (p. 98)? Given the situation, how serious is the criticism?

(d) Is Sheila's reaction mild or strong? Is she more tolerant than Harry?

(e) Why are Sheila and Harry more relaxed together after Jim and Jane have gone away (p. 99)?

2. How do Harry and Sheila make each other jealous?

(a) Sheila says 'Glad someone has some manners.' (p. 95). What is she suggesting?

(b) Why does Sheila say 'You'd do better to concentrate on the game.' and add 'Tennis.' (p. 96)?

(c) How does Harry criticize Sheila in front of Jane (pp. 93−94)?

(d) How does Sheila criticize Harry in front of Jim (p. 96, p. 97)?

3. In what ways are Harry and Sheila different from Jim and Jane?

(a) Compare Sheila's and Jane's appearance (pp. 93−94, p. 96, p. 99).

(b) Compare Harry's and Jim's job prospects (p. 99).

(c) What meaning is implied by Sheila's 'No . . .' (p. 99)?

(d) Sheila says Jim and Jane are 'mad about each other.' (p. 99). How would you describe Harry's and Sheila's feelings for each other?

4. In what way is the play concerned with the theme of winning and losing?

(a) What does Harry hope he will achieve by playing tennis with Jim (p. 96, p. 99)?

(b) Sheila says 'it's only a game.' (p. 97). Are their attitudes to the game different? In what way?

(c) Why is Harry so insistent about buying drinks (p. 98)?

(d) What tone of voice would you say Harry uses in his line, 'I really wasn't jealous when he was promoted − he deserved it.' (p. 99)

(e) Harry says 'there's more to life than that.' (p. 100). If Sheila asked 'What?', what would Harry reply?

Drama Activities

Choose *ONE* of these scenes. Prepare a dialogue in pairs and practise it within your own group. It may then be shown to the whole group.

1. After the game, Harry buys the drinks and starts to praise Jim's skill at tennis. He asks Jim to put in a good word for him at the office and suggests that all four have another game of tennis. Jim politely refuses both suggestions.

   Things to think about

   What sort of company do Jim and Harry work for?
   What jobs do they do?
   How soon did Jim get promotion?
   How long has Harry been doing the same job?

   USEFUL PHRASES FOR 1

   Marvellous game ... tremendous form ... absolutely unbeatable.

   Requests

   Do you think you could ...?
   I'd be very much obliged if you would ...

   Polite refusal

   Well, that's not so easy, you see ...
   Well, I am a bit busy at the moment.
   Why don't you ask ...?

   ---

2. At home after the match Jim and Jane discuss Harry and Sheila — Harry's ability at work, his attempt to get Jim to help him obtain a promotion, Sheila's appearance, Harry's and Sheila's behaviour on the tennis court, and Harry's request for another game. Jim and Jane decide not to see Harry and Sheila so often.

USEFUL PHRASES FOR 2

Do you know what he asked me?
I don't really enjoy playing tennis with them, it's such a walkover.
They're not very good, are they?
He really lost his temper.
I was so embarrassed.
I tried tactfully to suggest ...
He wouldn't take no for an answer.
They're not really our sort of people, are they?

---

3. The same tennis match, but this time the dialogue is between Jim and Jane. Write out their comments to each other, which Harry and Sheila cannot hear, and what they might say to Harry and Sheila at the net (do not give Harry's and Sheila's replies).

Staging

Take Harry's speech from 'Hell, really?' (p. 93) to '. . . it's what she does with it, poor darling.' (p. 94) Write down what Jim and Jane might be saying to Harry in the pauses. Decide from this how long the pauses would have to be in the original text.
Would Harry mime a ball falling onto his head (p. 98) or would you use a real ball?
If your audience do not know who Virginia Wade and Rod Laver are, which tennis champions would you put in their place?
What kind of look does Sheila give Harry at the end of the play?

Michael Frayn

Michael Frayn was born in London in 1933 and educated at Kingston Grammar School and Cambridge University. He became a reporter for the *Guardian* in 1957, and has also been a regular columnist for the *Observer*. Apart from his journalistic work, Frayn has written plays for stage and television as well as novels. His first novel, *The Tin Men* (1965), won the Somerset Maugham Award, and Frayn also received the Hawthornden Prize for Fiction in 1967 and the *Evening Standard* Best Comedy Award for the play *Alphabetical Order* in 1975. His plays, especially notable for their wit, include *The Two of Us* (1970), from which *Black and Silver* is taken, *The Sandboy* (1971), *Clouds* (1976), and two very popular recent plays: the farce, *Noises Off* (1982), which has enjoyed tremendous success both in London's West End and New York's Broadway, and a more serious social comedy, *Benefactors* (1984).

THE PLAY

A husband and wife take a second honeymoon in Venice, staying in the same room at the same hotel. The only difference this time is that they have a baby with them.

CHARACTERS

HUSBAND
WIFE

SETTING

A hotel bedroom in Venice.

BLACK AND SILVER

Night. HUSBAND *and* WIFE *are asleep. The window is open; reflections of lapping water move tranquilly up the wall outside. The curtain stirs in the night breeze. From somewhere in the distance there is a snatch of song. A church clock strikes three. It is followed by the sound of a small baby starting first to fret* and then to cry. At the first serious cry the* WIFE *starts up in bed, eyes still shut. She remains like that for a moment. The baby stops crying. The* WIFE'S *head falls back on to the pillow like a stone. A moment's silence, and then the baby starts to cry again. Once more the* WIFE *sits up in bed. This time she rubs her eyes and opens them; drags her hands down over her face; licks her lips; runs a weary hand through her hair. She sighs, and braces herself* with determination as if she is going to get up. Instead she drives her elbow into her* HUSBAND'S *back.*

WIFE: Your turn.

For a moment nothing happens. Then, in one complete delayed reflex action, the HUSBAND *rolls straight out of bed on to his feet and heads for the door of the bathroom, his eyes still shut. His* WIFE *falls back on the pillow, asleep.*

HUSBAND (*inarticulately,* his voice muscles still anaesthetized by sleep*): All right! Just going! Leave it to me! Sh!

A chair carrying the clothes stands between him and the door. He falls over it noisily. The WIFE *sits up in bed at once.*

WIFE (*whispering*): Sh! You'll wake the whole hotel!
HUSBAND (*blindly picking up himself and the chair, and piling the clothes back on to it.*): Sh! Relax! Leave it all to me! You're supposed to be having a holiday, remember.

He moves the chair out of harm's way, then opens the bathroom door and pulls out a carry-cot on a conveyor,* which he starts to push hurriedly back and forth. The crying stops and the WIFE *subsides on to her pillow again. The* HUSBAND, *whose eyes are still shut, and whose attitude suggests that* *he is trying to remain asleep on his feet, gradually ceases his pushing and creeps back to bed. When he gets to where the chair originally was, he stops and makes a careful detour,* which brings him up against it in its new position. Once again he falls over it; the baby cries; the* WIFE *starts up accusingly.*

HUSBAND: (*Putting the chair back into its original place, and returning to quiet the baby*): O.K.! Just going! Don't worry! Leave it to me! I'll fix it! Sh!

He pushes the carry-cot back and forth. The baby quietens.

WIFE: If you're going to go crashing about like this all night, you'd better put him back in the bathroom.

He wheels the cot into the bathroom, and emerges closing the door behind him. He heads back for bed, elaborately avoiding the chair in every possible position.

He is properly covered up, isn't he?

HUSBAND (*reassuringly**): Yes . . .

WIFE: You did check?

HUSBAND: Yes, yes.

He gets back into bed and settles down. A pause. The WIFE *is still sitting up, worrying.*

WIFE: Has he got a window open in there?

HUSBAND (*reassuringly, from the depths of the pillow*): Mm! Mm!

A pause.

WIFE: There aren't any windows in the bathroom.

HUSBAND (*explaining, without waking up*): Urm urmle urmurmurm . . .

WIFE: What?

HUSBAND (*wearily, taking his head out of the pillow*): I said no, but there's a ventilator.

A pause.

WIFE: Do you think he's getting enough vitamins?

Sighing, the HUSBAND *sits up and turns on the light.*

I mean, he brings up all his feed. He must bring up all the vitamins, too, mustn't he?

The HUSBAND *looks at his watch.*

HUSBAND (*pleadingly*): It's three o'clock!

Offended at the implied rebuke,* she turns away from him and lies down.

We're supposed to be on holiday! We're supposed to be getting some rest and relaxation!

WIFE: Rest and relaxation!

HUSBAND: What?

WIFE: How can I relax when everyone in the restaurant has to look the other way each time he brings his feed up?

HUSBAND: The *Italians* are all right — *they* don't mind him bringing his feed up. The Signora — all the girls who do the rooms — they think he's *marvellous*. It's all these English honeymoon couples. (*He turns the light out and lies down.*)

WIFE: Well, it wasn't my idea, coming back to Venice and getting the room we spent our honeymoon in.

HUSBAND: All they get at this hotel are honeymooners! I don't think they've ever seen a baby before, half of them!

WIFE: I feel like a spectre* at the feast, coming into the restaurant with the baby every morning.

HUSBAND: The *Italians* seem to think children are quite natural. '*E, bambolino! O, che bello ragazzo!* Can I hold him? *Eccolo! Bambolino, bambolino, bambolino!** Look — his little hands and foots! I keep him, yes?

His voice dies away. He has become aware that the baby is crying again. They both lie there, neither making the first move. Then the WIFE *sits up, sighing. At once the* HUSBAND *sits up, too — resignedly.**

All right! All right! I'm on duty.

He swings his legs out of bed. The WIFE *lies down again.*

He's stopped.

He swings his legs back into bed. Immediately the crying starts again. He swings his legs out of bed, walks slowly and aggrievedly towards the bathroom.

If you're going to be worn out every day, I suppose on holiday's as good a time as any . . .

He has reached the bathroom door, and is just about to open it, but realizes that the baby has stopped crying again. He stands stock still* for a moment, listening intently. Then he turns on his heel, and heads back towards the bed.

HUSBAND: The only thing that worries me is whether all this doesn't rather make a fool of one — whether it doesn't . . .

The crying starts again. The HUSBAND *freezes, and turns back towards the bathroom. The crying stops. He waits a moment, then heads back towards the bed.*

. . . weaken one's personality as . . .

He stops and swings back towards the bathroom, thinking to get a step ahead in the game. But the baby doesn't cry. He resumes his trip back to bed.

. . . as a father, in one's . . .

He gets into bed.

. . . relationship with the child . . .

The baby at once starts to cry. This time the HUSBAND *does nothing, except let his head sink into his hands. The* WIFE *sits up, exasperated,* as if the* HUSBAND *had never made an effort at all.*

WIFE: Are you going, or shall I?
HUSBAND (*wearily, getting up again*): No, no, no! Go to sleep. My round! I'm in the chair.

He trails to the bathroom, and pulls the carry-cot out, jiggling it back and forth as he does so. The crying dies away. The WIFE *subsides on to her pillow. Suddenly, he sniffs, and frowns. He stops pushing the cot back and forth; at which the baby starts to cry again; at which the* WIFE *sits up in bed. The* HUSBAND *doesn't notice her, however, because he is bending low over the cot, lifting the blanket within, and sniffing cautiously. He starts up hastily, whereupon the* WIFE *lies down again and feigns* immediate sleep. The* HUSBAND *silently curses his luck, then, automatically pushing the cot back and forth to quiet the baby, looks round at her and speaks ingratiatingly.**

Darling . . .!

There is no response. He goes over to her, dragging the cot, and his ingratiating tone becomes more urgent.

It's big jobs.

There is still no response. He shakes her uncertainly, undecided between firmness and gallantry.*

Well, that's damned funny, I must say. She was awake a moment ago.

The HUSBAND *turns to the cot and starts to remove the nappy.**

It's not that I *mind* doing it. It's just that I don't know where she keeps the stuff ... (*To the baby, in the special upbeat* tweedling* tones reserved for talking to babies*) Yes, it's old Dad who's on the job tonight, because lucky old Mum happens to be all tucked up in bed snoring her head off ...! Yes, she does ...! Oh, what a little stinky lad! What a little pooey-wooey ... uggy-puggy ... (*His increasing preoccupation with the difficulties of the operation makes his tone suddenly peremptory**) No, lie still! Lie *still*, blast you, or you'll get your feet in it. (*He looks round desperately, holding the baby's feet.*) Something to wipe you with ...

There is plainly nothing in sight. The baby gurgles contentedly. The HUSBAND *addresses it in his tweedling voice.*

It's all right for *you* to laugh! Yes, it's all right for *you* to laugh! I said it's all right for *you* to laugh ...! (*He looks desperately round again, returning to his more usual irritated adult tones.*) But what the flaming hell has she done with the Kleenex?* *I* don't know where she keeps things, do I, boy?

Still holding the baby's feet up with one hand, he peers into the bathroom.

She hides them all away in some godforsaken place, so I have to hold your bottom up in the air with one hand ...

He sees what he wants, high up inside the bathroom, and reaches off impossibly for it, still holding the baby's feet.

... and with the other ... do my best to ...

The sentence is completed by a cascading crash of falling objects, which makes the WIFE *sit up and put the light on, and brings her jumping out of bed and running to intervene.* She gazes into the bathroom at her* HUSBAND'S *efforts. He speaks defensively.*

HUSBAND: Well, fancy putting the Kleenex up on the topmost shelf!

WIFE: For God's sake! The whole of Venice must be awake by now!

HUSBAND   (*sarcastically*):   Do you usually change the baby up on the top shelf!

WIFE   (*fetching both Kleenex and a clean paper nappy from the wreckage in the bathroom*):   Go back to bed. I'll finish this.

HUSBAND   (*trying to keep her away from the cot*):   No, no, no — I'll do it. You're supposed to be having a holiday.

WIFE: Some holiday . . .

HUSBAND: Anyway, I'm doing it. You go back to bed and get some sleep.

WIFE: Sleep! I've forgotten what the word means! I wouldn't know it if I saw it! Come on, out of there.

She brushes him out of the way and finishes changing the baby.

HUSBAND   (*watching aggrievedly*):   I don't know why you're so eager all of a sudden.

WIFE   (*tweedlingly, to baby*):   Was it a nasty terrible surprise seeing that horrible Daddy man changing your nappy? (*Fiercely, to* HUSBAND) Because you make such a bloody meal of it!*

HUSBAND: *You* put the Kleenex out of reach!

WIFE   (*tweedingly, to baby*):   Is he keeping you awake, too, then, throwing all the jars of Nappisan* and all the packets of Bickiepegs* and all the little tins of Heinz strained spinach round the bathroom? (*Fiercely, to* HUSBAND) I don't know why you're so eager all of a sudden, come to that.

HUSBAND: Because I don't see why you should store up all the credit for changing his nappy when I've done all the dirty work already, that's why!

WIFE: This is the third time I've been up tonight.

HUSBAND: It's the third time *I've* been up.

WIFE: I was up most of last night.

HUSBAND: Who cleared up the mess in the Doge's Palace?*

WIFE   (*turning on him indignantly*):   I like that! What about the St. Mark's* incident . . .?

HUSBAND   (*suddenly conciliating**):   Oh, come on — let's not fight.

He sits down on the bed. The WIFE *turns back to finish the baby, agreeing to be slightly mollified.**

We had a great fight on our honeymoon. I can remember standing looking out of that window at the canal and thinking our marriage was over. I can't remember what we were arguing about, though. What on earth *did* we argue about before *he* was born? What did we talk about? What did we think about? We must have been bored out of our minds . . . Do you remember that day we went out to Torcello* and had a drink at the hotel where Hemingway used to stay? And you picked one of their geraniums and pinned it on my shirt . . .?

She turns to him, smiling slightly, and hands him the soiled nappy. He looks at it tenderly, rather as if it were a geranium, and puts his hands around hers.

WIFE: Put it down the lavatory for me, will you?
HUSBAND: Oh . . . Right.

He takes it out to the bathroom. She is just bending over the cot again when a sudden thought strikes her.

WIFE: Peter! Remember not to turn on the hot water!
HUSBAND *(off)*:   What?
WIFE: The hot water!

A colossal* thumping of air-locked plumbing fills the night. At once the baby starts to cry. The WIFE'S *head droops. She takes the baby out of the cot, wrapped up in its shawl,* and gets back into bed with it, cradling it. It stops crying. She turns out the light. The* HUSBAND *comes out of the bathroom, drying his hands. He seizes the cot and pushes it out to the bathroom, addressing a few encouraging words to the interior of the cot on the way.*

HUSBAND: Straight off to sleep now! There's a good boy!

The WIFE *dozes off. The* HUSBAND *executes a cunning retreat from the bathroom, then stands outside the door and listens. He smiles at the silence, and begins to creep away. But before he has gone more than a step or two he stops, frowning. He goes back and listens again. He frowns anxiously. He bends closer to the door and listens more intently. Then he pulls the cot out of the bathroom and puts*

his ear right down on top of it. He turns appalled* to his
WIFE, *and says in a terrible panic-stricken whisper*

HUSBAND: I think he's stopped breathing!

The WIFE *at once wakes with a start, and, still carrying the
baby, jumps out of bed and runs to join the* HUSBAND. *She
bends over the cot to listen.*

I mean, I don't want to wake him up if he *is* breathing . . .
WIFE (*urgently*):   Hold this . . .

She hands the baby to the HUSBAND, *and pulls back the
covers from the cot. She panics completely.*

Oh, my God, he's not there!

WIFE *and* HUSBAND *stare at each other for an instant in
horror. But at that moment the baby gives a cry, and they
both become aware of its whereabouts. The* WIFE *snatches it
out of the* HUSBAND'S *arms, with a look at him which
suggests that he was attempting to murder it. She hugs and
kisses it and puts it back into the cot. Reaction to their
shock makes them both furious.*

Stupid trick to play!
HUSBAND: Well, it wasn't my fault!
WIFE: Not breathing!
HUSBAND: Well, he *wasn't* breathing there — he was breathing
somewhere else!

They both get grumpily* back into bed. The WIFE *has pulled
the cot up to her side of the bed, so that she can keep jiggling
it back and forth as she lies there. The* HUSBAND *remains
sitting up in bed with his arms round his knees.*

Well, I'm wide awake now. I couldn't go to sleep if you paid
me . . .

There is no response from the WIFE.

You realize it's not breakfast time for another five hours
yet? You didn't pack any jigsaw puzzles,* did you?

*No response. A faint, rhythmic squeaking of springs
becomes audible.*

What's that?
WIFE: What?
HUSBAND: That squeak, squeak.

The WIFE *stops pushing the cot to and fro for a moment and listens.*

WIFE: Oh, that's the couple next door.

The HUSBAND *frowns, puzzled. Then light dawns.* *

HUSBAND: You mean, they've got a baby in there, too? Pushing it back and forth like us?

The WIFE *just looks at him.*

I thought they were all honeymoon couples in the hotel, apart from us?

The WIFE *goes on staring.*

Oh . . .! But at three o'clock in the morning?

WIFE: We probably woke them up. Anyway, why not?

HUSBAND: Well . . .! (*He thinks.*) I suppose we used to make love in the middle of the night, sometimes. Didn't we? I can't remember. It all seems so long ago.

WIFE: I can't remember what it was like at all before he was born.

HUSBAND: What did we do with all that time?

WIFE: We used to go to the cinema. Didn't we? Twice a week sometimes.

HUSBAND: We went out for meals in Chinese restaurants.

WIFE: We stayed in bed on Sundays . . .

The squeaking has ceased. The WIFE *stops jiggling the cot, and turns to the* HUSBAND.

Oh, Peter! What's happened to us? Have we changed? Have I changed? I have, haven't I?

HUSBAND (*reassuringly*): No, you haven't. (*He puts his arm round her.*)

WIFE: Do you still love me?

HUSBAND: Of course I do. (*He squeezes her affectionately.*)

WIFE: But not just out of habit? Not just out of a sense of duty?

HUSBAND (*stroking her head*): No!

WIFE: I still . . . you know . . . *attract* you?

He kisses her mouth, and silences her.

Even though I'm so preoccupied with him . . .

He kisses her again.

WIFE: ... and so ill-tempered and ...

He kisses her again, pressing her back on to the pillow.

... so on? (*She gazes up at him in silence.*) We'll have to be very quiet, then ...

Just as he is about to kiss her again, the baby starts to fret. They both freeze. The HUSBAND *looks round murderously at the cot.*

Oh ... Never mind! Go on!

The HUSBAND *continues to stare at the cot. The baby falls silent again. Slowly the* HUSBAND *turns back to kiss his* WIFE. *She puts her arm round him. Once again the baby begins to cry. Once again the* HUSBAND *looks round desperately. Without letting go of the* HUSBAND, *the* WIFE *stretches out her arm and begins to push the cot back and forth. The crying stops. Still pushing, she tries to encourage her* HUSBAND.

I love you!

HUSBAND   (*doing his best to concentrate on her*):   I love you!

WIFE: Go on, then! Don't stop!

But he turns to look at the cot, then disengages himself from her and sits up gloomily.

HUSBAND: I'll wait till you've got him back to sleep again.

He lies back against the pillows beside her. She sighs, and takes his hand.

WIFE: I'm sorry, love ... I'm sorry. I feel it's all my fault.

They lie side by side, gazing in front of them hand in hand, she pushing the cot back and forth. Gradually his head begins to loll, * *and his eyes close.*

Do you remember that day right at the end of the honeymoon, when we came back across the Lagoon in the twilight in that man's old motorboat, and the water was absolutely still — all black and silver, black and silver — and we dropped anchor and swam and the water was so warm and dark that you felt you could just let yourself go, and drift down into it forever ...?

WIFE (*She turns and sees that his eyes are shut*). You're not going to sleep? Are you?

His head slips a little further sideways.

I thought we were going to . . . Peter!

She prods him sharply. There is a momentary pause, and then, in one complete delayed reflex action, he rolls straight out of bed on to his feet, as at the beginning, and heads for where the cot was, his eyes still shut.

HUSBAND (*inarticulately*): All right! Just going! Sh! Leave it to me . . .!

BLACKOUT, *as he once again falls over the chair, and the baby cries.*

Glossary

The meanings given below are those which the words and phrases have as they occur in the play.

Page
107 *fret*: be discontented.
braces herself: prepares herself for something unpleasant.
inarticulately: speaking unclearly.
carry-cot on a conveyor: a light cot (box-like bed) for a baby, moved around on wheels.
108 *detour*: indirect route, way round something.
reassuringly: comfortingly.
109 *rebuke*: disapproval.
spectre: ghost.
'E, bambolino! O, che bello ragazzo!... Eccolo! Bambolino etc. (Italian): Hey, little doll! Oh, what a beautiful boy! ... There he is! Little doll etc.
resignedly: accepting calmly and without complaint.
110 *stock still*: motionless.
exasperated: very irritated.
feigns: imitates.
ingratiatingly: pleasantly, hoping to win favour.
111 *gallantry*: kindness shown by a man to a woman.
nappy: soft cloth worn around a baby's bottom and between its legs.
upbeat: cheerful, optimistic.
tweedling: bird-like, sounding like a bird.
peremptory: sharp, expecting to be obeyed immediately.
Kleenex: tissue paper.
intervene: stop something happening.
112 *make such a bloody meal of it*: make a difficult job of something quite easy.
Nappisan: powder used in water to sterilise dirty nappies.
Bickiepegs: brand name for teething biscuits.
Doge's Palace ... St Mark's: famous sights of Venice.
conciliating: being pleasant in order to calm anger or hostility.
113 *mollified*: soothed, less angry.
Torcello: an island near Venice.
colossal: very great.
shawl: soft garment worn by a woman around her shoulders or used to wrap around a baby.

114 *appalled*: deeply shocked.
 grumpily: in a bad temper.
 jigsaw puzzles: pictures cut up into small irregular pieces
 to be fitted together again for amusement.
115 *light dawns*: he realizes.
116 *loll*: hang down loosely.

Questions

> OUTLINE TO QUESTIONS
>
> 1. and 2. characterization: husband and
> wife
> 3. theme
> 4. theme

1. What differences in personality are there between the
 husband and wife?

   (a) Who do you expect will get up to see to the baby at the
    beginning (p. 107)? Who actually goes?
   (b) Why does the wife need reassuring (p. 108)?
   (c) It was the husband's idea to come for a second honey-
    moon to the same hotel (p. 109). What might that show
    about the differences in the couple's personalities?
   (d) Who appears to be better at taking care of the baby
    (pp. 111−113)?
   (e) What detail suggests that the husband is slower to
    realize things (p. 114)?

2. How is comedy produced through adults using baby talk?

   (a) What changes in tone take place when the husband and
    wife are changing the nappy? Are the changes gradual or
    sudden (pp. 111−113)?
   (b) Pick out examples of false good humour towards the
    baby (pp. 111−112). How do you know it is false?
   (c) How do both husband and wife use baby talk to attack
    each other (pp. 111−112)?

3. How does the play show the effect of a baby on marriage?

   (a) What does the husband mean when he wonders whether

'all this' weakens one's personality as a father in the relationship between father and child (p. 110)?

(b) What does the husband mean when he says they must have been bored out of their minds before the baby came (p. 113)?

(c) What changes in her personality does the wife feel have come about since the baby arrived (p. 115)?

4. How are the past and present contrasted?

(a) Sitting in the restaurant, how could the husband and wife not fail to think of their own honeymoon? Why is the situation now embarrassing rather than romantic (p. 109)?

(b) How is a contrast made between the day at Torcello and the present reality in the bathroom (p. 113)?

(c) Remembering the Lagoon, the wife imagines the feeling of drifting down into the water forever (p. 116). What type of mood or feeling is this? What is there about the words of this final speech that have made the husband fall asleep?

Drama Activities

Choose *ONE* of these scenes. Prepare a dialogue in pairs and practise it within your own group. It may then be shown to the whole group.

1. The couple plan their holidays. The husband wants to go back to Venice and get the same room in which they spent their honeymoon. His wife does not think this is a good idea. One of them gets their way.

USEFUL PHRASES FOR 1

Suggesting

Wouldn't it be wonderful to . . .?
We could . . .
Don't you think so?

USEFUL PHRASES FOR 1

Disagreement

Yes, but . . .
Well, perhaps, but . . .
To be honest, I don't agree.

Unwilling agreement

Oh, all right then.
Well, if you really want to.
Have it your own way, then.

2. A honeymoon couple at a nearby table are looking at the husband, wife and baby. One of the two thinks babies are sweet, the other can't stand them.

USEFUL PHRASES FOR 2

Opinions

Aren't they sweet?
Don't you think they're lovely?
Well, if you really want to know . . .
Well, if you ask me . . .

3. The sound of the baby crying wakes the couple up. There is an argument about who should take care of the baby this time.

USEFUL PHRASES FOR 3

Complaining

Are you going, or shall I?
Your turn.
I'm supposed to be having a holiday/getting some rest
  and relaxation.
It's all right for *you*.
Sleep! I've forgotting what the word means.
I've done all the dirty work.
This is the third time I've been up tonight.
I like that!
It wasn't my fault.

Staging

Draw a plan to show the bed, the chair, the bathroom and the bedroom light. Mark on it the movements of the two characters (you could use a different colour pen for each character).
Is the husband inside, outside or half way inside the bathroom when he is reaching for the Kleenex (p. 111)?
Would you have a wall to the bathroom and have the audience imagine what is happening there, or no bathroom wall and just a partition to suggest a door?
How would you make the beginning and end as similar as possible?

★　★　★　★　★

Score and Black and Silver: comparative questions

1. Is the role of visual comedy equally important in both plays? Give examples of visual comedy in both and say which you think is more effective and why.

2. Do you find the ideas of one play more interesting than those of the other? Why?

3. Both couples become angry with each other. Are both couples equally tolerant of each other? Is one member of the partnership more tolerant than the other?

4. What comparisons do both couples make between their own situations and those of other people?

SENTIMENT AND SENSATIONALISM

(Melodramas)

A. A. Milne

Alan Alexander Milne was born in London in 1882. He is known the
world over as a children's writer and as the creator of Winnie the Pooh
and Christopher Robin (the name, incidentally, of Milne's own son).
Milne's literary career was a varied one, however, for he was also a jour-
nalist, a dramatist, a novelist and a serious writer. He entered journal-
ism in 1903 after graduating from college, but it was not until three
years later that he finally established himself as a talented comic writer
on becoming Assistant Editor of the humorous magazine, *Punch*. He
remained with *Punch* until 1914 when he left to fight in the First World
War. After the war, Milne began writing one-act plays, together with a
number of full-length plays, among the most popular being the comedies
The Dover Road (1921) and *The Truth about Blayds* (1921), a mystery
play entitled *The Perfect Alibi* (1928) and *Toad of Toad Hall* (1929),
which remains to this day a great favourite with both adults and
children.

The Man in the Bowler Hat was first produced in New York in 1924.

THE PLAY

John and Mary, two of the most ordinary people in the world, are
spending a quiet evening at home as usual. Suddenly a gun shot
rings out and their sitting room becomes the scene of tremendous — if unlikely — drama.

CHARACTERS

JOHN
MARY
HERO
CHIEF VILLAIN
BAD MAN
MAN IN THE BOWLER HAT

THE MAN IN THE BOWLER HAT*

The Scene is MARY'S *sitting-room — the most ordinary sitting-room in the world.* JOHN *and* MARY, *two of the most ordinary people — he in the early forties, she in the late thirties — are sitting in front of the fire after dinner, He, as usual, is reading the paper; she, as usual, is knitting. They talk in a desultory* way.*

MARY: Did I tell you that Mrs. Patchett had just had another baby?

JOHN (*not looking up from his paper*): Yes, dear, you told me.

MARY: Did I? Are you sure?

JOHN: Last week.

MARY: But she only had it yesterday. Mr. Patchett told me this morning when I was ordering the cauliflower.*

JOHN: Ah! Then perhaps you told me she was going to have one.

MARY: Yes, I think that must have been it.

JOHN: This is the one that she was going to have?

MARY: It weighed seven pounds exactly.

JOHN: Of course, being a grocer, he would have the scales* ready. Boy or girl?

MARY: Boy.

JOHN: The first boy, isn't it?

MARY: The second.

JOHN (*sticking to it*): The first one that weighed seven pounds exactly.

They are silent again — he reading, she knitting.

MARY: Anything in the paper tonight?

JOHN (*turning over the paper*): A threatened strike of boiler-makers.

MARY: Does that matter very much?

JOHN: It says here that the situation is extremely serious.

MARY: Tell me about it.

JOHN (*not very good at it*): Well, the — er — boiler-makers are

125

threatening to strike. (*Weightily*)   They are threatening not
to make any more — er — boilers.

MARY: Kitchen boilers?

JOHN   (*with an explanatory gesture*):   Boilers. They are threatening not to make any more of them. And — well — that's
how it is. (*Returning to his paper*) The situation is extremely
serious. Exciting scenes have been witnessed.

MARY: What sort of scenes?

JOHN: Well, naturally, when you have a lot of men threatening
not to make any more boilers . . . and — er — a lot of other
men threatening that if they *don't* make any — well,
exciting scenes are witnessed. *Have* been witnessed by this
man, this special correspondent.

MARY   (*after a pause*):   It's a funny thing that nothing exciting
ever happens to *us*.

JOHN: It depends what you mean by exciting. I went round in
ninety-five* last Saturday — as I think I told you.

MARY: Yes, but I mean something really thrilling — and dangerous. Like in a novel — or on the stage.

JOHN: My dear Mary, nothing like that ever happens in real life.
I mean it wouldn't happen to *us*.

MARY: Would you like it if it did?

*He says nothing for a moment. Then he puts down his paper,
and sits there, thinking. At last he turns to her.*

JOHN   (*almost shyly*):   I used to imagine things like that
happening. Years ago. Rescuing a beautiful maiden and —
and all that sort of thing. And being wrecked on a desert
island* with her. . . . (*He turns away from her, staring into
his dreams.*) Or pushing open a little green door in a long
high wall, and finding myself in a wonderful garden under
the bluest of blue skies, and waiting, waiting . . . for something . . .

MARY: I used to imagine things too. People fighting duels*
because of me. . . . Silly, isn't it? Nothing ever really hapens
like that.

JOHN   (*still with his thoughts*):   No . . .

At this moment a STRANGE MAN *comes in. Contrary to all
etiquette,* * *he is wearing a Bowler Hat and an overcoat, and
has a half-smoked cigar in his mouth. He walks quickly
across the room and sits down in a chair with his back to the*

audience. JOHN *and* MARY, *deep in their thoughts, do not notice him.*

MARY (*looking into the fire*): I suppose we're too old for it now.
JOHN: I suppose so.
MARY: If it had only happened once — just for the memories.
JOHN: So that we could say to each other — Good lord! what's that?

It was the crack of a revolver. No mistaking it, even by JOHN, *who has never been much of a hand with revolvers.*

MARY (*frightened*): John!

There is a scuffling noise* outside the door. They look eagerly towards it. Then suddenly there is dead silence. The MAN IN THE BOWLER HAT *flicks some of his cigar ash on to the carpet* — MARY'S *carpet.*

JOHN: Look!

Very slowly the door begins to open. Through the crack comes a long, sinuous* hand. The door opens farther, and the hand is followed by a long, sinuous body. Still the MAN IN THE BOWLER HAT *says nothing. Then the door is closed, and leaning up against it, breathing rather quickly, is the* HERO, *in his hand a revolver.* JOHN *and* MARY *look at each other wonderingly.*

(*With a preliminary cough*) I — I beg your pardon!

HERO (*turning quickly, finger to his lips*): H'sh!
JOHN (*apologetically*): I beg your pardon!

The HERO *listens anxiously at the door. Then, evidently reassured for the moment, he comes towards them.*

HERO (*to* JOHN): Quick, take this!

He presses his revolver into JOHN'S *hand.*

JOHN: I — er — what do I . . .
HERO (*to* MARY): And you! This!

He takes another revolver from his hip-pocket and presses it into MARY'S *hand.*

MARY: Thank you. Do we . . .
HERO (*sternly*): H'sh!
MARY: Oh, I beg your pardon.
HERO: Listen!

They all listen. JOHN *and* MARY *have never listened so intently before, but to no purpose. They hear nothing.*

JOHN (*in a whisper*): What is it?

HERO: Nothing.

JOHN: Yes, that's what *I* heard.

HERO: Have you got a ... (*He breaks off and broods.* *)

MARY: A what?

HERO (*shaking his head*): No, it's too late now.

JOHN (*to* MARY): Haven't we got one?

MARY: I ordered one on Saturday, but it hasn't come.

HERO: You wait here — that will be best. I shall be back in a moment.

JOHN: What do we do?

HERO: Listen. That's all. Listen.

JOHN (*eagerly*): Yes, yes.

HERO: I shall be back directly.

Just as he is making for the window, the door opens and the HEROINE *— obviously — comes in. They stand gazing at each other.*

HEROINE: Oh! (*But with a world of expression in it.*)

HERO: Oh! (*With even more expression.*)

HEROINE: My love!

HERO: My beautiful!

They meet and are locked in an embrace.

JOHN (*to* MARY): I suppose they're engaged to be married.

MARY: Oh, I think they must be.

JOHN: They've evidently *met* before.

HERO (*lifting his head for a moment*): My Dolores! (*He bites her neck again.*)

JOHN (*to* MARY): I think this must be both 'How do you do' and 'Good-bye.'

MARY (*wistfully**): He is very good-looking.

JOHN (*casually*): Oh, do you think so? Now *she's* pretty, if you like.

MARY (*doubtfully*): Ye-es. Very bad style, of course.

JOHN (*indignantly**): My dear Mary ...

HEROINE (*to* HERO): Quick, quick, you must go!

HERO: Never — now that I have found you again.

HEROINE: Yes, yes! My father is hot upon your tracks.* He will be here at any moment in his two-seater.*

HERO (*turning pale*):   Your father!

HEROINE: I walked on ahead to warn you. He has come for — IT!

· JOHN (*to* MARY):   What on earth's IT?

HERO (*staggering*):   IT!

HEROINE: Yes.

JOHN (*to* MARY):   Income-tax collector.*

HERO: The Rajah's Ruby!*

MARY: Oh, how exciting!

HEROINE: Yes, he knows you have it. He is determined to wrest* it from you.

HERO: Never!

JOHN: Well done! Bravo! (*Offering his cigarette-case*) Would you care for a . . .

· *But the* HERO *spurns* * *it.*

HEROINE: There is no mischief he might not do, if once it were in his possession. Three prominent members of Society would be ruined, there would be another war in Mexico and the exchange value of the rouble* would be seriously impaired.* Promise me you will never give it up.

HERO: I promise.

HEROINE: I must go. I am betraying my father by coming here, but I love you.

JOHN (*to* MARY):   She does love him. I thought she did.

MARY: How could she help it?

HERO: I adore you!

JOHN: You see, he adores her too. It certainly looked like it.

MARY: I still don't think she's very good style.

HEROINE: Then — good-bye!

They embrace again.

JOHN (*after a decent interval*):   Excuse me, sir, but if you have a train to catch — I mean if your future father-in-law's two-seater is any good at all, oughtn't you to be — er . . .

HERO (*releasing* HEROINE):   Good-bye!

He conducts her to the door, gives her a last long lingering look, and lets her go.

MARY (*to herself*):   Pretty, of course, in a kind of way, but I must say I don't *like* that style.

The HERO *comes out of his reverie* and proceeds to business.*

HERO (*briskly to* JOHN): You have those revolvers?

JOHN: Yes.

HERO: Then wait here, and listen. More than one life depends upon it.

JOHN: How many more?

HERO: If you hear the slightest noise . . .

JOHN (*eagerly*): Yes?

HERO: H'sh!

He goes to the window, waits there listening for a moment, and then slips out. . . . JOHN *and* MARY *remain, their ears outstretched.*

JOHN (*with a start*): H'sh! What's that?

MARY: What was it, dear?

JOHN: I don't know.

MARY: It's so awkward when you don't quite know what you're listening *for*.

JOHN: H'sh! We were told to listen and we must listen. More than one life depends on it.

MARY: All right, dear.

They continue to listen. A little weary of it, MARY *looks down the barrel of the revolver to see if she can see anything interesting.*

JOHN (*observing her*): Don't do that! It's very dangerous to point a loaded revolver at yourself. If anything happened, it would be too late to say afterwards that you didn't mean it.

MARY: Very well, John — Oh, look!

Again the door opens quickly, and a sinister gentleman in a fur-coat inserts himself into the room. We recognize him at once as the CHIEF VILLAIN. *Very noiselessly, his back to* JOHN *and* MARY, *he creeps along the wall towards the window.*

JOHN (*in a whisper*): Father-in-law.

MARY: Do we . . . (*She indicates the revolver.*)

JOHN (*doubtfully*): I — I suppose . . . (*He raises his gun hesitatingly.*)

MARY: Oughtn't you to say something first?

JOHN: Yes — er . . . (*He clears his throat warningly.*) Ahem!

The CHIEF VILLAIN *continues to creep towards the window.*

You, sir!

MARY   (*politely*):   Do you want anything, or — or anything?

The CHIEF VILLAIN *is now at the window.*

JOHN: Just a moment, sir.

The CHIEF VILLAIN *opens the window and steps out between the curtains.*

MARY: Oh, he's gone!

JOHN: I call that very bad manners.

MARY: Do you think he'll come back?

JOHN   (*with determination*):   I shall shoot him like a dog if he does. (*Waving aside all protests*) Like a dog.

MARY: Yes, dear, perhaps that *would* be best.

JOHN: Look out, he's coming back.

He raises his revolver as the door opens. Again the CHIEF VILLAIN *enters cautiously and creeps towards the window.*

MARY   (*in a whisper*):   Shoot!

JOHN   (*awkwardly*):   Er — I suppose it *is* the same man?

MARY: Yes, yes!

JOHN: I mean — it wouldn't be quite fair if . . . (*He coughs warningly.*) Excuse me, sir!

The CHIEF VILLAIN *is now at the window again.*

MARY: Quick, before he goes!

JOHN   (*raising his revolver nervously*):   I ought to tell you, sir . . . (*To* MARY):   You know, I still think this is a different one.

The CHIEF VILLAIN *again disappears through the window.*

MARY   (*in great disappointment*):   Oh, he's gone!

JOHN   (*firmly*):   It was a different one. The other one hadn't got a moustache.

MARY: He had, John. It was the same man, of course it was.

JOHN: Oh! Well, if I had known that, if I had only been certain of it, I should have shot him like a dog.

A VOICE   (*which sounds like the* HERO'S):   Help, help!

MARY: John, listen!

JOHN: I *am* listening.

A VOICE: He-e-elp!

MARY: Oughtn't we to do something?

JOHN: We *are* doing something. We're listening. That's what he told us to do.

A VOICE: Help!

JOHN (*listening*): That's the other man, the one who came in first.

MARY: The nice-looking one. Oh, John, we *must* do something.

JOHN: If he calls out again, I shall — I shall — do something. I shall take steps. I may even have to.shoot somebody. But I will *not* have . . .

A VOICE: Quick, quick!

MARY: There!

JOHN: Er — was that the same voice?

MARY (*moving to the door*): Yes, of course it was. It sounded as if it were in the hall. Come along.

JOHN: Wait a moment. (*She turns round.*) We must keep cool, Mary. We mustn't be impetuous.* Just hold this a moment.

He hands her his revolver.

MARY (*surprised*): Why, what . . .

JOHN: I shall take my coat off. (*He takes off his coat very slowly.*) I'm going through with this. I'm not easily roused,* but when once . . .

A VOICE: Help! Quick!

JOHN (*reassuringly*): All right, my man, all right. (*Very leisurely he rolls up his sleeves.*) I'm not going to have this sort of thing going on in *my* house. I'm not going to have it. (*Doubtfully*) I don't think I need take my waistcoat* off too. What do *you* think, Mary?

MARY (*impatiently*): No, dear, of course not, you look very nice.

JOHN (*very determined*): Now, then, let's have that revolver. (*She gives it to him*) I shall say 'Hands up!' — very sharply, like that — '*Hands up!*' — and then if he doesn't put his hands up I shall — I shall say 'Hands up!' again. That will show him that I'm not to be trifled with.* Now then, dear, are you ready?

MARY (*eagerly*): Yes!

JOHN: Then . . .

But at that moment the lights go out.

MARY: Oh!

JOHN (*annoyed*): Now, why did you do that, Mary?

MARY: I didn't do it, dear.

JOHN: Then who did?

MARY: I don't know. They just went out.

JOHN: Then I shall write to the Company tomorrow and complain. I shall complain to the Company about the lights, and I shall complain to the landlord about the way people go in and out of this house, and shriek* and . . .

MARY (*in alarm*): Oh!

JOHN: *Don't* do that! What is it?

MARY: I can feel somebody quite close to me.

JOHN: Well, that's me.

MARY: Not you, somebody else. . . . Oh! He touched me!

JOHN (*addressing the darkness*): Really, sir, I must ask you not to . . .

MARY: Listen! I can hear breathings all round me!

JOHN: Excuse me, sir, but do you mind *not* breathing all round my wife?

MARY: There! Now I can't hear anything.

JOHN (*complacently*): There you are, my dear. You see what firmness does. I wasn't going to have *that* sort of thing going on in my house.

The lights go up and reveal the HERO *gagged* so that only his eyes are visible, and bound to a chair.*

MARY (*clinging to her husband*): Oh, John!

JOHN (*with sudden desperate bravery*): Hands up! (*He levels his revolver.*)

MARY: Don't be silly, how can he?

JOHN: All right, dear, I was only practising. (*He blows a speck of dust off his revolver, and holds it up to the light again.*) Yes, it's quite a handy little fellow. I think I shall be able to do some business with this all right.

MARY: Poor fellow! I wonder who it is.

The HERO *tries to speak with his eyes and movements of the head.*

JOHN: He wants something. Perhaps it's the evening paper. (*He makes a movement towards it.*)

MARY: Listen!

The HERO *begins to tap with his feet.*

JOHN: He's signalling something.

MARY: Dots and dashes!*

JOHN: That's the Morse Code,* that's what that is. Where's my dictionary?

He fetches it hastily and begins to turn over the pages.

MARY: Quick, dear!

JOHN (*reading*): Here we are. '1. Morse — The walrus.'* (*Looking at the* HERO.) No, that must be wrong. Ah, this is better. '2. Morse code signalling of telegraph-operators — as "He sends a good morse".'

MARY: Well? What does it say?

JOHN: Nothing. That's all. Then we come to 'Morsel — a small piece of food, a mouthful, a bite. Also a small meal.'

MARY (*brilliantly*): A mouthful! That's what he means! He wants the gag taken out of his mouth.

She goes to him.

JOHN: That's very clever of you, Mary. I should never have thought of that.

MARY (*untying the gag*): There! ... Why it's the man who came in first, the nice-looking one!

JOHN: Yes, he *said* he was coming back.

Before the HERO *can express his thanks — if that is what he wants to express — the* CHIEF VILLAIN, *accompanied by a* BAD MAN, *comes in.* JOHN *and* MARY *instinctively retreat.*

CHIEF VILLAIN (*sardonically**): Ha!

JOHN (*politely*): Ha to you, sir.

The CHIEF VILLAIN *fixes* JOHN *with a terrible eye.*

(*Nervously to* MARY): Say 'Ha!' to the gentleman, dear.

MARY (*faintly*): Ha!

CHIEF VILLAIN: And what the Mephistopheles* are *you* doing here?

JOHN (*to* MARY): What *are* we doing here?

MARY (*bravely*): This is our house.

JOHN: Yes, this is *our* house.

CHIEF VILLAIN: Then siddown!*

> JOHN *sits down meekly.* *

Is this your wife?

JOHN: Yes. (*Making the introduction*) Er — my wife — er — Mr — er — the gentleman . . .

CHIEF VILLAIN: Then tell her to siddown too.

JOHN (*to* MARY): He wants you to siddown.

> *She does so.*

CHIEF VILLAIN: That's better. (*To* BAD MAN) Just take their guns off 'em.

BAD MAN (*taking the guns*): Do you want them tied up or gagged or anything?

CHIEF VILLAIN: No, they're not worth it.

JOHN (*humbly*): Thank you.

CHIEF VILLAIN: Now then, to business. (*To* HERO) Where's the Rajah's Ruby?

HERO (*firmly*): I shan't tell you.

CHIEF VILLAIN: You won't?

HERO: I won't.

CHIEF VILLAIN: That's awkward. (*After much thought*) You absolutely refuse to?

HERO: I absolutely refuse to.

CHIEF VILLAIN: Ha! (*To* BAD MAN) Torture* the prisoner.

BAD MAN (*cheerfully*): Right you are, governor.* (*He feels on the lapel* of his coat and then says to* MARY) Could you oblige me with the loan of a pin, Mum?

MARY: I don't think . . . (*Finding one*) Here you are.

BAD MAN: Thanks.

> *He advances threateningly upon the prisoner.*

CHIEF VILLAIN: Wait! (*To* HERO) Before proceeding to extremities, I will give you one more chance. Where is the Rujah's Raby?

BAD MAN: You mean the Rabah's Rujy, don't you, governor?

CHIEF VILLAIN: That's what I said.

JOHN (*wishing to help*): You *said* the Rubah's Rajy, but I think you meant the rhubarb's . . .

CHIEF VILLAIN: Silence! (*To* HERO) I ask you again — where is the Ruj — I mean where is the Rab . . . Well anyhow, where *is* it?

HERO: I won't tell you.

CHIEF VILLAIN: Proceed, Mr. Smithers.

BAD MAN: Well, you've asked for it, Mate.

He pushes the pin into the HERO'S *arm.*

HERO: Ow!

MARY: Oh, poor fellow!

CHIEF VILLAIN: Silence! Where is . . .

The HERO *shakes his head.*

Torture him again, Mr. Smithers.

HERO: No, no! Mercy! I'll tell you.

JOHN (*indignantly*): Oh, I say!

BAD MAN: Shall I just give him another one for luck, governor?

HERO: Certainly not!

JOHN (*to* MARY): Personally I think he should have held out much longer.

CHIEF VILLAIN: Very well, then. Where is the Rajah's Ruby?

HERO: In the cloak-room* of Waterloo Station.* In a hat-box.

CHIEF VILLAIN (*doubtfully*): In the cloak-room at Waterloo Station, you say?

HERO: Yes. In a hat-box. Now release me.

CHIEF VILLAIN: How do I know it's there?

HERO: Well, how do *I* know?

CHIEF VILLAIN: True. (*Holding out his hand*) Well, give me the ticket for it.

HERO: I haven't got it.

BAD MAN: Now then, none of that.

HERO: I haven't really.

JOHN: I don't think he'd say he *hadn't* got it, if he *had* got it. Do you, Mary?

MARY: Oh, I'm sure he wouldn't.

CHIEF VILLAIN: Silence! (*To* HERO) Where is the ticket?

HERO: In the cloak-room of Paddington Station.* In a hat-box.

CHIEF VILLAIN: The same hat-box?

HERO: Of course not. The other one was at Waterloo Station.

CHIEF VILLAIN: Well, then, where's the ticket for the hat-box in the Paddington cloak-room?

HERO: In the cloak-room at Charing Cross. In a hat-box.

CHIEF VILLAIN (*annoyed*): Look here, how many hat-boxes have you got?

HERO: Lots.

CHIEF VILLAIN: Oh! Now let's get this straight. You say that the Rajah's Ruby is in a hat-box in the cloak-room at Paddington . . .

HERO: Waterloo.

CHIEF VILLAIN: Waterloo; and that the ticket for that hat-box is in a hat-box in the cloak-room at Euston . . .

HERO: Paddington.

CHIEF VILLAIN: Paddington; and that the ticket for this ticket, which is in a hat-box at Paddington, for the Ruby which is in a hat-box at King's Cross . . .

BAD MAN: Euston.

JOHN (*tentatively*): St. Pancras?

MARY: Earl's Court?

CHIEF VILLAIN (*angrily*): Oh, shut up! The ticket for this ticket, which is in a hat-box at Paddington, for the Ruby which is in a hat-box at — at . . .

HERO: Waterloo.

CHIEF VILLAIN: Waterloo, thank you. This ticket is in a hat-box at — er . . .

JOHN (*with decision*): St. Panrcas.

MARY (*equally certain*): Earl's Court.

CHIEF VILLAIN: *Shut up!* In a hat-box at . . .

HERO: Charing Cross.

CHIEF VILLAIN: Exactly. (*Triumphantly*) Then give me the ticket!

HERO: Which one?

CHIEF VILLAIN (*uneasily*): The one we're talking about.

JOHN (*helpfully*): The St. Pancras one.

MARY: The Earl's Court one.

CHIEF VILLAIN (*in a fury*): *Will* you shut up? (*To* HERO) Now listen. (*Very slowly and with an enormous effort of concentration*) I want the ticket for the hat-box at Charing Cross, which contains the ticket for the hat-box at . . .

JOHN'S *lips indicate 'St. Pancras' to* MARY, *whose own seem to express a preference for Earl's Court. The* VILLAIN *gives them one look, and goes on firmly.*

— at Paddington, which contains the ticket for the hat-box

at Waterloo, which contains the Rajah's Ruby. (*Proudly*)
There!

HERO: I beg your pardon?

CHIEF VILLAIN (*violently*): I will *not* say it again! Give me the
ticket!

HERO (*sadly*): I haven't got it.

CHIEF VILLAIN (*in an awe-struck whisper*): You haven't got
it?

HERO: No.

CHIEF VILLAIN (*after several vain attempts to speak*): Where
is it?

HERO: In the cloak-room at Victoria Station.

CHIEF VILLAIN (*moistening his lips and speaking faintly*): Not
— not in a hat-box?

HERO: Yes.

CHIEF VILLAIN (*without much hope*): And the ticket for that?

HERO: In the cloak-room at Euston.

CHIEF VILLAIN (*quite broken up**): Also in a hat-box?

HERO: Yes.

CHIEF VILLAIN: How much longer do we go on?

HERO (*cheerfully*): Oh, a long time yet.

CHIEF VILLAIN (*to* BAD MAN): How many London stations are
there?

JOHN: Well, there's St. Pancras, and . . .

MARY: Earl's Court . . .

BAD MAN: About twenty big ones, governor.

CHIEF VILLAIN: Twenty. (*To* HERO) And what do we do when
we've gone through the lot?

HERO: Then we go all round them again.

CHIEF VILLAIN (*anxiously*): And — and so on?

HERO: And so on.

CHIEF VILLAIN (*his hand to his head*): This is terrible. I must
think. (*To* BAD MAN) Just torture him again while I think.

BAD MAN (*cheerfully*): Right you are, governor.

He approaches his victim.

HERO (*uneasily*): I say, look here!

JOHN: I don't think it's quite fair, you know . . .

MARY (*suddenly*): Give me back my pin!

BAD MAN: Must obey orders, gentlemen. (*Coaxingly to* HERO)
Just a little way in! (*Indicating with his fingers.*) That much.

JOHN   (*to* MARY):   I think perhaps 'that much' wouldn't matter. What do . . .

CHIEF VILLAIN   (*triumphantly*):   I've got it!

He rises with an air, the problem solved. They all look at him.

JOHN: What?

CHIEF VILLAIN   (*impressively to* HERO):   There is somewhere — logically, there must be somewhere — a final, an ultimate hat-box.

JOHN: By Jove!* That's true!

HERO: Yes.

BAD MAN   (*scratching his head*):   I don't see it.

CHIEF VILLAIN: Then — where *is* that hat-box?

JOHN   (*cheerfully*):   St. Pancras.

MARY: Earl's Court.

CHIEF VILLAIN: Shut up! (*To* HERO) Where is that hat-box?

HERO: In the cloak-room at Charing Cross.

CHIEF VILLAIN: Ah! (*He holds out his hand.*) Then give me the ticket for it.

BAD MAN   (*threateningly*):   Come on now! The ticket!

HERO   (*shaking his head sadly*):   I can't.

CHIEF VILLAIN   (*almost inarticulate with emotion*):   You don't mean to say you've — lost — it?

HERO   (*in a whisper, with bowed head*):   I've lost it.

With a terrible shriek the CHIEF VILLAIN *falls back fainting into the arms of the* BAD MAN.

Instinctively JOHN *and* MARY *embrace, sobbing to each other*:   He's lost it!

The HEROINE *rushes in, crying*:   My love, you've lost it! *and puts her arms round the* HERO.

Only the MAN IN THE BOWLER HAT *remains unmoved. Slowly he removes the cigar from his mouth and speaks.*

BOWLER HAT: Yes. . . . That's all right. . . . Just a big ragged* still. . . . We'll take it again at eleven tomorrow. . . . Second Act, please.

And so the rehearsal goes on.

Glossary

The meanings given below are those which the words
and phrases have as they occur in the play.

Page
125   *bowler hat*:   hard, rounded hat for men, traditionally worn
by London office-workers.
desultory: moving randomly from one topic to another.
cauliflower: a type of vegetable.
scales: instrument for weighing.

126   *I went round in ninety-five*:   this refers to an extremely
poor score at golf.
wrecked on a desert island: stranded on a remote island
after one's ship has been destroyed (e.g. by storm) at sea.
duels: fights with pistols or swords between two people
to decide a question of honour.
etiquette: formal rules of behaviour.

127   *scuffling noise*:   noise of struggling or fighting.
sinuous: not stiff, snake-like.

128   *broods*:   thinks seriously and sadly.
wistfully: sadly, longingly.
indignantly: angrily.
hot upon your tracks (coll.):   close behind you.

129   *two-seater*:   car with seats for two people.
Income-tax collector: suggested by the initials 'i' and 't'
in 'IT'.
Rajah's Ruby: precious jewel, deep red in colour,
belonging to an Indian prince.
wrest: take by force.
spurns: refuses with angry pride.
exchange value of the rouble: the value of Soviet Union
money in relation to money used in other countries. (The
rouble is not, in fact, exchanged internationally.)
impaired: weakened.

130   *reverie*:   dreamy, pleasant thoughts.

132   *impetuous*:   rash, too hasty.
roused: made angry, angered into action.
waistcoat: a close-fitting garment without sleeves worn
under a man's jacket.
trifled with: treated as unimportant.

133   *shriek*:   scream loudly.
gagged: with something tied over his mouth to silence
him.

134   *Dots and dashes ... Morse Code*:   a telegraphic system of

short sounds (dots) and long sounds (dashes) to represent letters of the alphabet when signalling.

walrus: a large seal-like animal with two long upper teeth (also called 'the morse').

sardonically: scornfully.

Mephistopheles: a rather unusual and pompous way of saying 'Devil'. (Mephistopheles was the Devil to whom Faust sold his soul in German legend.)

135 *siddown* (coll.): sit down.

meekly: quietly, without protesting.

Torture: cause great physical pain to.

governor (coll.): boss, chief.

lapel: the folded part of the front of a coat which continues from the collar.

136 *cloak-room*: place in a station where belongings (bags etc.) may be left and picked up later.

Waterloo Station, Paddington Station etc.: the stations mentioned on the following pages are all London railway stations, except Earl's Court, which is an underground station.

138 *broken up*: emotionally destroyed.

139 *By Jove*: a rather old-fashioned exclamation of surprise, meaning 'By God'.

ragged: rough at the edges.

Questions

OUTLINE TO QUESTIONS

1. genre/characterization: John and Mary
2. genre/characterization: Hero and Heroine
3. genre/characterization: Hero, Chief Villain, Bad Man, John, Mary
4. genre

---

1. How do John and Mary provide a humorous contrast between the world of adventure and the ordinariness of real life?

    (a) How quickly do we realize that John and Mary are *'two of the most ordinary people in the world'* (p. 125)? Give examples.

(b) Where do we discover that even they have a need for adventure and romance (p. 126)?

(c) Where does the 'adventurous' part of the play begin (p. 127)?

(d) What possible explanation could be given for the gun shot (p. 127)?

(e) Give some examples of inappropriate remarks made by John and Mary whilst the Hero and Heroine are kissing (p. 128).

(f) John does not seem to think the Hero is particularly good-looking and Mary says the Heroine is 'Very bad style.' (p. 128). Why?

2. How are the conventions of young romantic love made fun of through the parts of the Hero and Heroine?

(a) Is much said by the young couple when the Heroine first arrives (p. 128)?

(b) From the Heroine's words (pp. 128–129), it is clear that the Hero has a powerful enemy. Who is this? Why is such a person a very typical enemy for a young lover to have?

(c) Where does Milne make fun of badly written melodrama in which much of the plot has to be told directly to the audience (p. 129)?

(d) The traditional way of acting out melodrama is to say the lines 'out front', that is, directly to the audience and not to the person you are supposed to be talking to. What comic effects are achieved by playing the scene between Hero and Heroine 'out front' (pp. 128–129)?

3. In what ways does Milne reverse the traditional characteristics of good, bad and ordinary characters?

(a) Is the Hero always very brave (p. 136)?

(b) Is the Chief Villain always powerful and frightening (p. 135, p. 138)?

(c) The Bad Man asks for a pin (p. 135). In what way is it unusual for a supposedly 'Bad Man' to ask for something in this way?

(d) Are John and Mary always kind and sympathetic to sufferers (pp. 135–136)?

4. How concerned is Milne with dramatic and psychological realism?

    (a) Is the gun shot (p. 127) ever explained or made part of the action?

    (b) Is there ever an explanation of how the Hero was bound and gagged and put in the sitting room (p. 133)?

    (c) Are any of the parts believable characters from every-day life? Are even John and Mary very ordinary (see question 3d)?

    (d) Is it clear whether the Hero is tricking the Chief Villain with his details about railway stations or whether he is telling the truth (Milne's stage directions for the Hero's last two lines give a clue, p. 139)? Which alternative is funnier?

    (e) Is the Man in the Bowler Hat given any special character? Would the play be better or worse without him?

Drama Activities

Prepare these sketches and practise them within your own groups. They may then be shown to the whole group.
Sketch 1. should be prepared in pairs; 2. and 3. in groups of four.

1. Start off a *very ordinary* conversation between a middle-aged married couple.

    Situation

    Watching television, or woman knitting/man reading the newspaper.

    Conversation

    Something you have heard yourself/ the recent birth of Mrs Patchett's baby/ something the man is reading about in the newspaper/ something that is on television (you choose).

    Starter (woman)

    Did I tell you that . . .?
    Anything in the paper tonight . . .?
    What's on the box?

2. Start off as with 1 above. Enter the daughter of the family with a young man. After a time the daughter (or young man) tells the family that they are going to get married. This is the first time that the family have met the young man and they are surprised. Father disapproves, but mother is very pleased. Develop this situation in any way you like.

   This improvisation should be played as *realistically* as possible.

   Decide what sort of people the older couple are, how old they are, whether they are working or retired etc.

   The young man can be a shy university student/arrogant with shocking hair-style and clothes/a policeman etc.

   The daughter should be determined and proud of the young man. Decide what the daughter does (student/unemployed/junior manageress etc.)

3. Start off like 2 above, but develop *melodramatically* (a secret reason why the couple should never marry/a guilty secret of the father or mother etc.).

   End the scene with some sort of dramatic resolution.

SOME MELODRAMATIC PHRASES

But you can't do this to me/us!
How could you do this?
Haven't we always treated you right?
I can't say how disturbed you've made me feel.
Where did we go wrong?
There's nothing for it, I shall have to . . .
If that is truly the way you feel, then . . .
Oh, that it should come to this!

Staging

What colour clothes should the Hero, Heroine, Chief Villain and Bad Man wear?
Where should Mary and John be seated?
Where should the Hero and Heroine stand in relation to them?
Should the Man in the Bowler Hat be plainly visible to the audience when he is seated?

Which characters should be played 'out front' in an exaggerated manner (see question 2d), and which should be played more realistically?

Should the Chief Villain see John and Mary when he twice enters their living room (p. 131)?

How intelligent should such characters as the Hero, the Chief Villain and the Bad Man appear to be?

How swift should the action and dialogue be?

Richard Dennis

Richard 'Johnny' Dennis was born in London in 1940 and sees himself as an 'actor who writes the odd sketch'. He has had a long and happy association with The Players Theatre, which is the leading Music Hall Company in the world and tours Britain and the USA, and he has enjoyed working in close contact with other actors and producers. His three published sketches all make fun of traditional melodrama. They are *Maria Marten* (1970), *The Bells* (1973), written with Michael Kilgarriff, and *Tram Track Tragedy* (1977).

MARIA MARTEN OR MURDER IN THE RED BARN

On May 18, 1827, William Corder, a local landowner from the east of England, shot and killed his mistress, a country girl called Maria Marten, in a farm building known as the Red Barn. Here Corder buried her, and perhaps his crime would never have been discovered had Maria's mother not had a dream showing where her daughter was buried. Corder was tried, repented his crime and was hanged on August 18, 1828. Almost immediately, many theatrical versions of this real-life event appeared, and it became perhaps the most popular of all Victorian melodramas. It had all the right ingredients — a wicked upper class squire, a poor misused country girl and a murder — and, of course, the facts that did not fit the picture, such as Maria's two illegitimate children, conceived before she met Corder, were conveniently forgotten.

The version of *Maria Marten* printed here was written in 1970 in the style of the Music Halls. The Music Hall was a type of theatrical entertainment, popular in Britain in the nineteenth and early twentieth centuries, which specialized in comedy and song. A Chairman introduced all the events and would encourage the audience to join in the songs and, if there was a melodrama, get them to hiss the villain and cheer the heroine — though the audience needed little or no encouragement. Occasionally, members of the audience would shout out witty comments to the performers on the stage.

Richard Dennis's version of *Maria Marten* succeeds in turning the tragedy and sentimentality of the original Victorian melodrama into fun and laughter.

THE SKETCH

The Chairman sets the scene for the terrible murder of Maria Marten at the hands of the wicked William Corder.

CHARACTERS

CHAIRMAN
MARIA MARTEN: a poor village girl
SQUIRE WILLIAM CORDER: a villain
A VOICE
THE STAGE-MANAGER (non-speaking)

MARIA MARTEN
or
MURDER IN THE RED BARN

CHAIRMAN: Ladies and gentlemen, it is, as you well know, the tradition of this house to present only the very finest artistes;* it gives me therefore the greatest pleasure to be able to announce that our stage is now to be graced by the presence of two of England's leading Thespians* — and when I say England's leading Thespians I mean of course the world's leading Thespians — Sir Herbert and Lady Beerbohm Bush!* These distinguished luminaries* of the theatrical profession have graciously consented tonight to give us two scenes from that celebrated spine-chiller:* *Maria Marten*, or *Murder in The Red Barn.*

Loud chords from the orchestra.

(*Testily* *) Not yet — not yet.
> Our heroine will first appear;
> Her name's Maria — so give her a cheer!

MARIA *enters R, curtseys* * to the audience, wafts a gracious kiss to the* CHAIRMAN *and departs L.*

> Here's William Corder, the wicked squire;*
> Please hiss and boo this villain dire!*

CORDER *sweeps on L, with a big smile over his evil features. His confident entrance is spoiled by the boos and hisses which greet him: his smile vanishes and he responds by hissing back at the audience. He wraps his coat round him in a defiant gesture and exits R, scowling.* *

I will now call upon our stage-manager to set the scene.

The Tabs * open.*

The STAGE-MANAGER* *enters R, carrying a card bearing the words 'Maria's Kitchen'. He is very nervous and shakes visibly. However, under the* CHAIRMAN'S *encouragement —
who invites the audience to applaud him — he bucks up* *and*

147

displays his card all around with growing enthusiasm. Indeed, it quickly becomes apparent that he is loth* to leave the stage, and the CHAIRMAN *has tactfully to wave him off.*

Yes, thank you — yes, very good. Thank you so much . . .

The STAGE-MANAGER *exists R.*

So now, the scene is set and the artistes are waiting in the wings.* Ladies and Gentlemen, *Maria Marten* or *Murder In The Red Barn.* (*Aside to the orchestra*) Now! (*He sits.*)

Crashing chords from the orchestra, changing to sweet heroine theme ('O Star of Eve' from 'Tannhäuser') as . . .

MARIA *enters L.*

MARIA (*in despair*): Oh! Oh! Oooh!
A VOICE (*either off-stage or from out front*): Oh — get on with it!
MARIA (*recovering swiftly*): Oh, that I Maria Marten, a poor village gel,* was wronged by the Squire William Corder. And did not the child of our union die of some strange illness? (*Happily*) But he shall marry me. I hold his promise here.

She reaches into her bodice,* realizes the note is not there. She turns her back on the audience and removes it from the top of her stocking.

I hold his promise here. Oh, but once I was an innocent maiden — now what am I? (*She weeps.*)

VOICE: I could tell you!
MARIA: But hark — I hear his footsteps. (*She puts her hand to her L ear. Silence.*) But hark — I hear his footsteps.

CORDER *enters R.*

CORDER (*as he enters*): Ha ha!

Lights flash, the music plays crashing minor chords, and the following-spot changes momentarily to green. Hisses from the audience are returned by CORDER *before he addresses* MARIA.

(*To* MARIA, *taking her hand; evilly*): Dearest Maria!
MARIA: Oh William, you have come at last!
CORDER: On receiving your note I came to you at once!

MARIA   (*breaking from him a little*):   When are you going to keep the promise you made to me?

CORDER: I come to tell you that the death of my father removes the only obstacle to our union.

MARIA: I shall tell my parents at once.

She crosses him, but he catches her by her left arm.

CORDER: One moment, Maria, you know the aversion* me* mother has to your family. Therefore I wish the marriage to be performed — in *London*!

Music: 'Do not trust him, gentle maiden!'

MARIA: In London! Why there?

CORDER: Business requires me to leave at once. Therefore I wish you to meet me tonight — in the *Old Red Barn*!

Thunderous chords. Lights flash on and off.

MARIA: No, no! Anything but the Old Red Barn!

CORDER   (*leering* and twirling his moustache*):   Anything?

MARIA   (*submitting to her fate*):   The Old Red Barn . . .

CORDER   (*stroking her hand*):   Do not worry, Maria, for from the Barn we shall start on our road to love and happiness.

Music reprises:* 'Do not trust him'.

MARIA: Very well, I consent, and shall meet you tonight at the Old Red Barn!

MARIA *exits R, smiling bravely.*

The music immediately crashes into a minor chord.*

CORDER   (*laughing triumphantly*):   Ha — ha!

MARIA *returns momentarily to blow him a kiss.*
CORDER *recovers quickly and by rapid facial gymnastics manages to give her a twisted smile.*
MARIA *exits.*

(*Returning to his normal scowling self*): She consents! Curse the gel! She binds me down — me mad gambling debts have left me penniless. Only a rich marriage can save me now. Maria, when you consented to meet me in the Old Red Barn, you sealed your doom!*

Music fortissimo — perhaps the opening of Beethoven's Sonata Pathetique. Lights flash.

CORDER, *with a flourish of his cloak, strides to exit R, The*
STAGE-MANAGER *enters and there is a collision.* CORDER *is
furious at having his grand exit ruined, and slides off
ignominiously* in high dudgeon.**

The STAGE-MANAGER, *quite confident this time, has another
sign to display. This one reads 'The Old Red Barn', and
though it is shown round with the greatest of aplomb,* it is
unfortunately upside down. Shouts of 'Upside down!' from
the audience and the wings only serve to confuse him. He
turns upstage and checks his fly-buttons,* at which the*
CHAIRMAN *gently indicates the cause of the trouble. The*
STAGE-MANAGER *is in no way put out; he simply turns the
sign right way up and shows it round as before. Again the*
CHAIRMAN *has to get him off stage tactfully by applauding
and encouraging the audience to do the same.*
At last the STAGE-MANAGER *exits R.*

*The lights lower and the music recommences, very sinister
and foreboding;* again perhaps the Beethoven could be
played.*

CORDER *enters, stops and looks round to see if the coast is
clear. To make sure, he strides round the stage in a big circle,
and as he passes the R entrance a hand comes out holding a
shovel. Without looking at it or breaking step,* CORDER *takes
it and continues to C. He mimes digging.*

On the first thrust of CORDER'S *shovel there is a chord of
music, then another as he throws the earth over his shoulder.
This is repeated once, then* CORDER *moves to the R entrance,
but the chords are played a third time.* CORDER *looks at the
orchestra with hatred and mouths 'Fool!' At the R entrance
a hand comes out and takes the shovel.*

CORDER: All is completed! I await now my victim — will she
come? Oh yes, a woman will do anything for the man she
loves. Hark! I hear her footsteps now tripping across the
fields.

Off R are heard ponderous,* thudding footsteps.

She has a song on her lips.

We hear Maria screeching 'Nellie Dean.'*

Little does she know that death is so near!

He goes up L and draws his cloak up over his face.

The lights come up to full, and Maria's theme music is heard.
MARIA *enters R.*

MARIA: William! William! (*Moving down C*) Not here?

She backs upstage to where CORDER *is concealed.*
As MARIA *nears him,* CORDER *lifts the cloak as if about to smother* her. This usually gets a good response from the audience of 'Look out!' and 'Behind you!' At the last moment* MARIA *moves RC, and* CORDER *almost overbalances.*

Oh, how frightening it is here alone! I will leave this place at once . . .

CORDER   (*revealing himself*):   Stay, Maria! (*He moves to her.*)
MARIA: Oh William, how glad I am to see you. Let us leave this horrible place at once. (*She moves to exit R.*)
CORDER   (*grabbing her L wrist*):   One moment — did anyone see you cross the fields?
MARIA   (*wondering*):   No one.
CORDER   (*chuckling*):   That's good. Maria, do you remember a few days ago threatening to betray me about our child to Constable* Ayers?
MARIA   (*with a light laugh*):   Oh William . . .

She sweeps her L hand across expansively,* and inadvertently* catches CORDER *in the stomach.* CORDER *folds.*

. . . a foolish jest!*

Another gesture catches his top hat and rams* it over his ears as he rises.
MARIA *is oblivious,* but* CORDER *is furious.*

Let us leave this place.

CORDER   (*straightening his hat*):   No, no! Do you think my life is to be held at the bidding of a silly gel? No — look what I have made here! (*He indicates where he has been digging.*)
MARIA: What is it?
CORDER   (*very big*):   A grave!

A chord of music.

I mean to kill you and bury your body here.
MARIA: Oh, no!
CORDER: You are a clog* on me actions, a chain . . . (*He mimes pulling a chain.*) . . . that stops me reaching ambitious heights. You are to die — tonight!

MARIA (*weeping at his feet*): No, not by your hand, the hand that loved me. Oh, spare me! Spare me!

CORDER: 'Tis useless! Me mind's resolved. You die tonight!

MARIA (*rising*): Wretch, since neither pity nor love will save me, Heaven will surely nerve* my arm to battle for my life!

Chase music. CORDER *and* MARIA *struggle, their hands interlocked in a stylized manner.*

CORDER: Foolish gel! Desist!* (*He throws her from him L.*)

MARIA: Never whiles I live! (*She moves in to renew the fight.*)

CORDER: Then you die! (*He throws her L again and takes out a gun.*)

The music stops. CORDER *pulls the trigger. There is no sound.*

Then you die!

He pulls the trigger again, and again there is no sound. CORDER *turns to go off R to see what has happened to the gunshot; he takes only two steps when the shot fires offstage.* MARIA *clasps her bosom and staggers across RC.* CORDER *turns on his heels and runs to catch her, misses, turns again in time to catch her and lay her gently on the stage. The lights begin to lower and the music plays sadly. ('Hearts and Flowers' is the usual choice here, but the slow movement from Beethoven's Sonata Pathetique may be preferred. It is especially effective if a violinist is available.*)

MARIA: William, I am dying — your cruel hand has stilled the heart that loved you. Death claims me — but with my last breath I die blessing and forgiving thee. (*Her head droops.*)

CORDER *gently lays her flat. The music stops.* CORDER *rises, takes one step, and raises a hand and opens his mouth to speak, when* MARIA *revives.* (*Ideally she should speak as* CORDER'S *foot is actually in the air.*)

I die! (*She drops again.*)

CORDER *looks at her, then tries again. Again she revives.*

I die! (*She drops.*)

CORDER *tries a third time, and stops himself to look at her. She does not move.*

CORDER (*angry, but controlling himself for his final big speech*): Blessings and forgiveness for me, her murderer? (*He looks*

at her face.) Oh Maria, do not look so tenderly upon me. Let
fire burn from your lips and curse me.

> Oh, may my crime for ever stand accursed,
> The last of murders as it is — the worst!

CORDER *exits in a swirl of cloak. The* CURTAIN *falls, or there
is a Black-out, to crashing minor chords.*

   *The music changes to "The Soldiers' March" from
'Carmen' as the* CURTAIN *rises and the lights come up to full.
The* STAGE-MANAGER *enters and helps* MARIA *to her feet and
the two of them graciously take bows.* CORDER *comes on and
pushes the* STAGE-MANAGER *out of the way. The* STAGE-
MANAGER *goes to the other side of* MARIA *and continues
taking bows as though he had just given the finest Lear* of
the century.*

CURTAIN

Note: *If there is no* CURTAIN *and the actors have to walk off
in sight of the audience,* CORDER *should try to be the last one
off stage, but somehow the* STAGE-MANAGER *takes the last
call, waving and blowing kisses to his public.*

Glossary

The meanings given below are those which the words and phrases have as they occur in the sketch.

Page
147   *artistes*:   professional public performers.

Thespians: actors, especially tragic actors (Thespis was a Greek poet of the sixth century B.C.).

Sir Herbert and Lady Beerbohm Bush: a joke on the name of Sir Herbert Beerbohm Tree (1853–1917), a famous actor and manager in his day, who frequently appeared on the stage with his wife.

luminaries: leading lights, famous people.

spine-chiller: something that makes you terrified.

Testily: irritably.

curtseys: bends her knee and lowers her head.

squire: the main landowner in a rural community.

villain dire: very evil man.

scowling: looking angry.

Tabs: curtains.

Stage-Manager: person in charge of the theatre stage during a performance.

bucks up: cheers up, becomes happier.

148   *loth*:   unwilling.

wings: the sides of the stage where actors are hidden from view.

gel: spelling used to indicate the pronunciation of the word 'girl' by the British upper class (William Corder also says 'gel'). Perhaps Maria is trying here to sound more refined than she really is.

bodice: upper part of a woman's dress.

149   *aversion*:   strong dislike.

me: British upper class way of saying 'my'.

leering: smiling an unpleasant smile that expresses thoughts of sex.

reprises: repeats.

minor chord: combination of musical notes which have a serious and dramatic sound.

sealed your doom: made your death certain.

150   *ignominiously*:   defeated and shamed.

in high dudgeon: in a state of very bad temper.

aplomb: self-confidence.

fly-buttons: trouser buttons.

foreboding:　indicating that something bad is about to happen.

ponderous:　slow and heavy.

'Nellie Dean':　a popular old-fashioned British song.

151　*smother*:　choke, prevent from breathing.

Constable:　policeman.

expansively:　with a large movement.

inadvertently:　accidentally.

jest:　joke.

rams:　pushes down hard.

oblivious:　unaware.

clog:　obstruction, something that prevents freedom.

152　*nerve*:　give courage to.

Desist:　stop.

153　*Lear*:　Shakespeare's tragic hero, King Lear.

Questions

> OUTLINE TO QUESTIONS
>
> 1. genre
> 2. genre/characterization: Corder and Maria
> 3. genre/themes
> 4. genre

1. What features of the Music Hall (see p. 146) are found in this version of *Maria Marten*?

   (a) How does the Chairman encourage the audience to join in (p. 147)?
   (b) Where is music used and what effect does it have?
   (c) In what way does the Voice from the audience (p. 148) add to the comedy?

2. How is the high seriousness of Victorian melodrama made fun of in the comic version of *Maria Marten*?

   (a) Is the actor taking the part of Corder a professional or an amateur actor (p. 148)? Do the other actors seem to be amateurs or professionals?

(b) How is the seriousness of the part of Corder destroyed by the Stage-Manager (p. 150), the orchestra (p. 150) and Maria (p. 151)?

(c) What features of Maria show her to be a rather unsuitable heroine (p. 148, pp. 150—151)?

(d) Is there any part of the play where there is genuinely serious emotion?

3. Here are some common themes found in Victorian melodrama. Which of these themes appear in Dennis's version of *Maria Marten*? Give examples.

(a) A wicked villain from the upper classes seduces an innocent maiden.

(b) The wicked city/the goodness of the countryside.

(c) Repentance.

(d) Justice.

(e) Class differences.

(f) The death of an innocent child.

(g) Fate.

4. Is Dennis's version of *Maria Marten* concerned with dramatic realism?

(a) In Dennis's sketch the Chairman, like all Music Hall Chairmen, introduces the main performers. Why does this not normally happen in plays seen at the theatre? Why does it happen in Music Hall?

(b) For approximately how much of the sketch are Maria and Corder alone and speaking directly to the audience? Is this common in most plays today? What sort of information are they giving the audience?

(c) How is Corder given a shovel (p. 150)? Why is he given it in this way?

(d) Why are the entrances of the Stage-Manager necessary? How are changes of scene usually made in most plays today?

Drama Activities

Choose *ONE* of these scenes. Prepare it and practise it within your own group. The scenes may be either comic or serious, and may be shown to the whole group. Where appropriate, scenes may be joined together to form a continuous class performance.

Scenes 1. and 2. should be prepared in groups of three; 3. and 4. in pairs; 5. in groups of three to five.

1. Maria's parents try to persuade her never to see Corder again.

2. Corder's parents try to persuade him never to see Maria again.

3. The murder in the Red Barn following the action of Dennis's version of *Maria Marten*, but this time performed tragically and seriously.

4. Maria's mother tells her husband of the dream she has had which shows her where Maria's body is buried. Maria's father thinks at first it is only a dream but is at last persuaded to see if it is true.

5. The trial of William Corder. At first Corder pronounces his innocence, but after the evidence is presented — the shovel, the gun, the discovery of the grave — he confesses his guilt and repents his crime. The judge sentences him to death.
   Roles: William Corder
   The Judge
   The Lawyer for the Prosecution
   The Lawyer for the Defence (if wished)
   Maria's mother as witness (if wished)

Staging

What colour clothes should Maria and Corder wear?
How realistic or exaggerated should the acting be?
What could be done to make sure the audience joins in when the Chairman encourages them to hiss and boo?
Could the play be successfully performed without (a) music (b) lighting (c) a gun (d) the role of the Stage-Manager? If so, what alterations would you make? Would you make any further alterations to make the action funnier for your local audience?

The Man In The Bowler Hat and Maria Marten: comparative questions

1. Which play do you find funnier and why?

2. Music Hall died out in the late 1920s because it could not compete with the popularity of the cinema. Do you find any similarities between either of the plays and old silent movies or modern-day melodramatic plays and films?

3. In both plays the heroine is rather helpless. Are the heroines of modern plays, books and films so helpless?

4. To what extent are both Milne's and Dennis's dramas 'plays within plays'?

5. In Dennis's sketch, Maria is at the centre of the action; in Milne's play, the Heroine is not. Write or perform a scene from *The Man in the Bowler Hat* in which there is a confrontation between the Heroine and the Chief Villain.

NEGLECT
(Absurdist Plays)

Alan Ayckbourn

Alan Ayckbourn was born in London in 1939, and since the age of seventeen has been actively engaged in the theatre. After a series of acting parts with local theatres in England, he joined the Studio Theatre at Scarborough where he developed as an actor and especially as a playwright. Today Ayckbourn is one of the most successful and popular dramatists writing in Britain, but he still retains strong roots with the seaside town of Scarborough. It is there that his plays are first performed, tried and tested, before coming to London's West End theatres. Ayckbourn seems to write best when he puts himself under certain restrictions. He admits that the process of writing plays is hard and painful work, so he often begins writing at tremendous speed and pressure shortly before rehearsals are due. Secondly, Ayckbourn enjoys setting himself certain technical problems. His play *Absurd Person Singular* (1972), for example, is divided into three acts which show, using the same cast, three parties on three consecutive Christmas Eves, skilfully charting the rise of one couple and the fall of the other two. Similarly, his series of three plays, *The Norman Conquests* (1974), show the events of one weekend in the country from three interlinking but different points of view. Ayckbourn's plays, which could be called 'comedies of manners', put in a clear and comic light the frustrations and self-imposed problems of the British middle class.

Among his plays not already mentioned are *Relatively Speaking* (1967), *Confusions* (1976), from which *Mother Figure* is taken, *Just Between Ourselves* (1977) and *Intimate Exchanges* (1984).

THE PLAY

Lucy is a housewife with three young children. She never answers the phone, always wears a dressing gown and has not left the house in weeks. Rosemary, a neighbour, comes round to deliver a message, and finds Lucy's behaviour rather odd.

CHARACTERS

LUCY
ROSEMARY
TERRY

MOTHER FIGURE

LUCY'S *sitting-room. It is a suburban room, fairly untidy, with evidence of small children. There are two doors — one to the kitchen and back door, one to the bedrooms and front door.*

LUCY *hurries in from the bedrooms on her way to the kitchen. She is untidy, unmade-up, in dressing-gown and slippers.*

LUCY (*calling behind her*): Nicholas! Stay in your own bed and leave Sarah alone.

The telephone rings. LUCY *goes out to the kitchen, returning at once with a glass of water.*
All right, Jamie, darling. Mummy's coming with a dinkie* . . .

As she passes the telephone, she lifts the receiver off the rest and almost immediately replaces it.

Mummy's coming, Jamie, Mummy's coming.

LUCY *goes off to the bedroom with the glass. The front door chimes* sound. A pause, then they sound again.* LUCY *returns from the bedrooms.*

Sarah! You're a naughty, naughty girl. I told you not to play with Jamie's syrup. That's for Jamie's toothipegs* . . .

The door chimes sound again. LUCY *ignores these and goes off to the kitchen. She returns almost at once with a toilet roll, hauling off handfuls of it as she goes to perform some giant mopping-up operation.*

Nicholas, if you're not in your bed by the time I come up, I shall smack your botty.*

There are two rings on the back door bell. LUCY *goes off to the bedroom. A pause.* ROSEMARY, *a rather frail,* mousey-looking* woman, comes in from the kitchen.*

ROSEMARY (*calling timidly*): Woo-hoo!

LUCY *returns from the bedroom.*

LUCY (*calling as before*): Now go to sleep. At once. (*Seeing* ROSEMARY) Oh.

ROSEMARY: Hallo. I thought you must be in.

LUCY (*puzzled*): Hallo?

ROSEMARY: I thought you were in.

LUCY: Yes.

ROSEMARY: You are.

LUCY: Yes.

ROSEMARY: Hallo.

LUCY: Hallo. (*A slight pause.*) Who are you?

ROSEMARY: Next door.

LUCY: What?

ROSEMARY: From next door. Mrs Oates. Rosemary. Do you remember?

LUCY (*vaguely*): Oh, yes. Hallo.

ROSEMARY: Hallo. I did ring both bells but nobody seemed . . .

LUCY: No. I don't take much notice of bells.

ROSEMARY: Oh.

LUCY: I've rather got my hands full.

ROSEMARY: Oh yes. With the children, you mean? How are they?

LUCY: Fine.

ROSEMARY: All well?

LUCY: Yes.

ROSEMARY: Good. It's three you've got, isn't it?

LUCY: Yes.

ROSEMARY: Still, I expect it's time well spent.

LUCY: I haven't much option.*

ROSEMARY: No.

LUCY: Well.

ROSEMARY: Oh, don't let me — if you want to get on . . .

LUCY: No.

ROSEMARY: I mean, if you were going to bed.

LUCY: Bed?

ROSEMARY (*indicating* LUCY'S *attire**): Well . . .

LUCY: Oh, no. I didn't get dressed today, that's all.

ROSEMARY: Oh. Not ill?

LUCY: No.

ROSEMARY: Oh.

LUCY: I just wasn't going anywhere.

ROSEMARY: Oh, well . . .

LUCY: I haven't been anywhere for weeks.

ROSEMARY: That's a shame.

LUCY: I don't think I've got dressed for weeks, either.

ROSEMARY: Ah. No, well, I must say we haven't seen you. Not that we've been looking but we haven't seen you.

LUCY: No. Do you want to sit down?

ROSEMARY: Oh, thank you. Just for a minute.

LUCY: If you can find somewhere. (*She moves the odd toy.*)

ROSEMARY (*sitting*): Yes, we were wondering if you were alright, actually. My husband and I — Terry, that's my husband — he was remarking that we hadn't seen you for a bit.

LUCY: No.

ROSEMARY: We heard the children, of course. Not to complain of, mind you, but we heard them but we didn't see you.

LUCY: No.

*She picks up various toys during the following and puts them in the play-pen.**

ROSEMARY: Or your husband.

LUCY: No.

ROSEMARY: But then I said to Terry, if they need us they've only to ask. They know where we are. If they want to keep themselves to themselves, that's all right by us. I mean, that's why they put up that great big fence so they could keep themselves to themselves. And that's all right by us.

LUCY: Good.

ROSEMARY: And then ten minutes ago, we got this phone call.

LUCY: Phone call?

ROSEMARY: Yes. Terry answered it — that's my husband — and they say will you accept a transfer charge call* from a public phone box in Middlesbrough* and Terry says, hallo, that's funny, he says, who do we know in Middlesbrough and I said, not a soul and he says, well, that's funny, Terry says, well who is it? How do we know we know him? If we don't know him, we don't want to waste money talking to him but if we do, it might be an emergency and we won't sleep a wink.* And the operator says, well suit yourself, take it or leave it, it's all the same to me. So we took it and it was your husband.

LUCY: Harry?

ROSEMARY: Harry, yes. Mr Compton.

LUCY: What did he want?

ROSEMARY: Well — you. He was worried. He's been ringing you for days. He's had the line checked but there's been no reply.

LUCY: Oh.

ROSEMARY: Has it not been ringing?

LUCY: Possibly. I don't take much notice of bells.

She goes to listen for the children.

ROSEMARY: Oh. Anyway, he sounded very worried. So I said I'd pop round* and make sure. I took his number in case you wanted to . . .

LUCY is clearly not listening.

Are you all right?

LUCY: Yes, I was listening for Nicholas.

ROSEMARY: Oh. That's the baby?

LUCY: No.

ROSEMARY (*warmly**): Ah.

LUCY: I'm sorry. I'm being very rude. It's just I haven't — spoken to anyone for days. My husband isn't home much.

ROSEMARY: Oh, I quite understand. Would you like his number?

LUCY: What?

ROSEMARY: Your husband's telephone number in Middlesbrough. Would you like it? He said he'd hang on.* It's from a hotel.

LUCY: No.

ROSEMARY: Oh.

LUCY: Whatever he has to say to me, he can say to my face or not at all.

ROSEMARY: Ah. (*Laying a slip of paper gingerly* on the coffee-table*) Well, it's there.

LUCY: Would you care for a drink or something?

ROSEMARY: A drink? Oh — well — what's the time? Well — I don't know if I should. Half past — oh yes, — why not? Yes, please. Why not? A little one.

LUCY: Orange or lemon?

ROSEMARY: I beg your pardon?

LUCY: Orange juice or lemon juice? Or you can have milk.

ROSEMARY: Oh, I see. I thought you meant . . .

LUCY: Come on. Orange or lemon? I'm waiting.

ROSEMARY: Is there a possibility of some coffee?

LUCY: No.

ROSEMARY: Oh.

LUCY: It'll keep you awake. I'll get you an orange, it's better for you.

ROSEMARY: Oh . . .

LUCY *(as she goes)*: Sit still. Don't run around. I won't be a minute.

LUCY *goes out into the kitchen.*

ROSEMARY *sits nervously. She rises after a second, looks guiltily towards the kitchen and sits again. The door chimes sound.* ROSEMARY *looks towards the kitchen. There is no sign of* LUCY. *The door chimes sound again.* ROSEMARY *gets up hesitantly.*

ROSEMARY *(calling)*: Mrs — er . . .

LUCY *(off, in the kitchen)*: Wait, wait, wait! I'm coming . . .

The door chimes sound again. ROSEMARY *runs off to the front door.* LUCY *returns from the kitchen with a glass of orange juice.*

Here we are, Rosemary, I . . . *(She looks round the empty room, annoyed. Calling)* Rosemary! It's on the table.

LUCY *puts the orange on the coffee-table and goes out to the kitchen again.* ROSEMARY *returns from the hall with* TERRY, *a rather pudgy* man in shirt sleeves.*

ROSEMARY *(sotto voce*)*: Come in a minute.

TERRY: I'm watching the telly.

ROSEMARY: Just for a minute.

TERRY: I wondered where you'd got to. I mean, all you had to do was give her the number . . .

ROSEMARY: I want you to meet her. See what you think. I don't think she's well.

TERRY: How do you mean?

ROSEMARY: She just seems . . .

TERRY: Is she ill?

ROSEMARY: I don't know . . .

TERRY: Well, either she's ill or she isn't.

ROSEMARY: Ssh.

LUCY *returns from the kitchen with a plate of biscuits.*

LUCY: Here we are now. (*Seeing* TERRY) Oh.

TERRY: Evening.

LUCY: Hallo.

ROSEMARY: My husband.

LUCY: Terry, isn't it?

TERRY: Yes.

LUCY: That's a nice name, isn't it? (*Pointing to the sofa*) Sit down there then. Have you got your orange juice, Rosemary?

TERRY *sits*

ROSEMARY: Yes, thank you.

She picks up the glass of orange juice and sits.

TERRY: Orange juice?

ROSEMARY: Yes.

TERRY: What are you doing drinking that?

ROSEMARY: I like orange juice.

LUCY: Now, here's some very special choccy bics* but you mustn't eat them all. I'm going to trust you.

She starts tidying up again.

ROSEMARY (*still humouring her*): Lovely. (*She mouths 'say something' to* TERRY.)

TERRY: Yes. Well, how are you keeping then — er, sorry, I'm forgetting. Lesley, isn't it?

LUCY: Mrs Compton.

TERRY: Yes. Mrs Compton. How are you?

LUCY: I'm very well, thank you, Terry. Nice of you to ask.

TERRY: And what about Har — Mr Compton?

LUCY: Very well. When I last saw him. Rosemary dear, try not to make all that noise when you drink.

ROSEMARY: Sorry.

TERRY: Yes, we were saying that your husband's job obviously takes him round and about a lot.

LUCY: Yes.

She starts folding nappies. *

TERRY: Doesn't get home as much as he'd like, I expect.

LUCY: I've no idea.

TERRY: But then it takes all sorts. Take me, I'm home on the nose* six o'clock every night. That's the way she wants it. Who am I . . .? (*Pause.*) Yes, I think I could quite envy your husband, sometimes. Getting about a bit. I mean, when you think about it, it's more natural. For a man. His natural way of life. Right back to the primitive. Woman stays in the cave, man the hunter goes off roving at will.* Mind you, I think the idea originally was he went off hunting for food. Different sort of game these days, eh?

ROSEMARY (*hissing*): Terry!

TERRY: Be after something quite different these days, eh? (*He nods and winks.*)

LUCY: Now don't get silly, Terry.

TERRY: What? Ah — beg your pardon.

A pause. TERRY *munches* a biscuit.* ROSEMARY *sips her orange juice.*

ROSEMARY: Very pleasant orange juice.

LUCY: Full of vitamin C.

TERRY: No, I didn't want to give you the wrong impression there. But seriously, I was saying to Rosie here, you can't put a man in a cage. You try to do that, you've lost him. See my point?

LUCY: That can apply to women, too, surely?

ROSEMARY: Yes, quite right.

TERRY: What do you mean, quite right?

ROSEMARY: Well . . .

TERRY: You're happy enough at home, aren't you?

ROSEMARY: Yes, but — yes — but . . .

TERRY: Well then, that's what I'm saying. You're the woman, you're happy enough at home looking after that. I'm the man, I have to be out and about.

ROSEMARY: I don't know about that. You'd never go out at all unless I pushed you.

TERRY: What do you mean? I'm out all day.

ROSEMARY: Only because you have to be. You wouldn't be if you didn't have to be. When you don't, you come in, sit down, watch the television and go to bed.

TERRY: I have to relax.

ROSEMARY: You're always relaxing.

TERRY: Don't deny me relaxing.

ROSEMARY: I don't.

ROSEMARY: Yes, you do, you just said . . .

LUCY: Now, don't quarrel. I won't have any quarrelling.

TERRY: Eh?

ROSEMARY: Sorry.

LUCY: Would you like an orange drink as well, Terry? Is that what it is?

TERRY: Er . . . Oh no — I don't go in for that sort of drink much, if you know what I mean. (*He winks, then reaches for a biscuit*). I'll have another one of these though, if you don't mind?

LUCY: Just a minute, how many have you had?

TERRY: This is my second. It's only my second.

LUCY: Well, that's all. No more after that. I'll get you some milk. You'd better have something that's good for you.

TERRY (*half rising*): Oh no — thank you, not milk, no.

LUCY (*going to the kitchen*): Wait there. (*Seeing* TERRY *has half risen*) And don't jump about while you're eating, Terry.

LUCY *goes out to the kitchen.*

TERRY: You're right. She's odd.

ROSEMARY: I said she was.

TERRY: No wonder he's gone off.

ROSEMARY: Perhaps that's why she's odd.

TERRY: Why?

ROSEMARY: Because he's gone off.

TERRY: Rubbish. And we'll have less of that, too, if you don't mind.

ROSEMARY: What?

TERRY: All this business about me never going out of the house.

ROSEMARY: It's true.

TERRY: It's not true and it makes me out to be some bloody idle loafer.*

ROSEMARY: All I said . . .

TERRY: And even if it is true, you have no business saying it in front of other people.

ROSEMARY: Oh, honestly, Terry, you're so touchy.* I can't say a thing right these days, can I?

TERRY: Very little. Now you come to mention it.

ROSEMARY: Niggle,* niggle, niggle. You keep on at me the whole time. I'm frightened to open my mouth these days. I don't know what's got into you lately. You're in a filthy mood* from the moment you get up till you go to bed . . .

TERRY: What are you talking about?

ROSEMARY: Grumbling and moaning . . .

TERRY: Oh, shut up.

ROSEMARY: You're a misery to live with these days, you really are.

TERRY: I said, shut up.

ROSEMARY (*more quietly*): I wish to God you'd go off somewhere sometimes, I really do.

TERRY: Don't tempt me. I bloody feel like it occasionally, I can tell you.

ROSEMARY (*tearfully*): Oh, lovely . . .

TERRY: If you think I enjoy spending night after night sitting looking at you . . . (*He throws the biscuit down.*) What am I eating these damn things for . . . you're mistaken.

Thirsty from the biscuits, he grabs her orange juice glass and drains it in one.*

ROSEMARY: That's mine, do you mind. (*She rises and stamps her foot.*)

TERRY: Come on. Let's go. (*He jumps up.*)

ROSEMARY: That was my orange juice when you've quite finished.

LUCY *enters with a glass of milk.*

LUCY: Now what are you doing jumping about?

ROSEMARY *sits.*

TERRY: We've got to be going, I'm sorry.

LUCY: Not till you've finished. Sit down.

TERRY: Listen, I'm sorry we . . .

LUCY (*seeing* ROSEMARY'S *distraught* state): What's the matter with Rosemary?

ROSEMARY (*sniffing*): Nothing . . .

TERRY: Nothing.

LUCY: What have you been doing to her?

TERRY: Nothing.

LUCY: Here's your milk.

TERRY: Thank you.

LUCY: You don't deserve it.

TERRY: I don't want it.

LUCY: Don't be tiresome.

TERRY: I hate the damned stuff.

LUCY: I'm not going to waste my breath arguing with you,
Terry. It's entirely up to you if you don't want to be big and
strong.

TERRY: Now, look . . .

LUCY: If you want to be a little weakling, that's up to you. Just
don't come whining* to me when all your nails and teeth fall
out. Now then, Rosemary, let's see to you. (*She puts down
the milk and picks up the biscuits.*) Would you like a choccy
biccy?

ROSEMARY: No, thank you.

LUCY: Come on, they're lovely choccy, look. Milk choccy . . .

ROSEMARY: No, honestly.

TERRY: Rosie, are you coming or not?

LUCY: Well, have a drink, then. Blow your nose and have a
drink, that's a good girl. (*Seeing the glass*) Oh, it's all gone.
You've drunk that quickly, haven't you?

ROSEMARY: I didn't drink it. He did.

LUCY: What?

ROSEMARY: He drank it.

LUCY: Terry, did you drink her orange juice?

TERRY: Look, there's a programme I want to watch . . .

LUCY: Did you drink Rosemary's orange juice?

TERRY: Look, good night . . .

ROSEMARY: Yes, he did.

LUCY: Well, I think that's really mean.

ROSEMARY: He just takes anything he wants.

LUCY: Really mean.

ROSEMARY: Never thinks of asking.

TERRY: I'm going.

LUCY: Not before you've apologized to Rosemary.

TERRY: Good night.

TERRY *goes out.*

LUCY (*calling after him*): And don't you dare come back until
you're ready to apologize. (*To* ROSEMARY) Never mind him.
Let him go. He'll be back.

ROSEMARY: That's the way to talk to him.

LUCY: What?

ROSEMARY: That's the way he ought to be talked to more often.

LUCY: I'm sorry. I won't have that sort of behaviour. Not from anyone.

ROSEMARY: He'll sulk* now. For days.

LUCY: Well, let him. It doesn't worry us, does it?

ROSEMARY: No. It's just sometimes — things get on top of you — and then he comes back at night — and he starts on at me and I . . . (*She cries.*) Oh dear — I'm so sorry — I didn't mean to . . .

LUCY (*cooing*): Come on now. Come on . . .

ROSEMARY: I've never done this. I'm sorry . . .

LUCY: That's all right. There, there.

ROSEMARY: I'm sorry. (*She continues to weep.*)

LUCY: Look who's watching you.

ROSEMARY: Who?

LUCY (*picking up a doll*): Mr Poddle. Mr Poddle's watching you. (*She holds up the doll.*) You don't want Mr Poddle to see you crying, do you? Do you?

ROSEMARY (*lamely**): No . . .

LUCY: Do we, Mr Poddle? (*She shakes Mr Poddle's head.*) No, he says, no. Stop crying, Rosie. (*She nods Mr Poddle's head.*) Stop crying, Rosie. Yes — yes.

ROSEMARY *gives an embarrassed giggle.*

That's better. Was that a little laugh, Mr Poddle? Was that a little laugh?

LUCY *wiggles Mr Poddle about, bringing him close up to* ROSEMARY'S *face and taking him away again.*

Was that a little laugh? Was that a little laugh? Was that a little laugh?

ROSEMARY *giggles uncontrollably.* TERRY *enters from the hall and stands amazed.*

TERRY: Er . . .

LUCY *and* ROSEMARY *become aware of him.*

Er — I've locked myself out.

LUCY: Have you come back to apologize?

TERRY: You got the key, Rosie?

ROSEMARY: Yes.

TERRY: Let's have it then.

LUCY: Not until you apologize.

TERRY: Look, I'm not apologizing to anyone. I just want the key. To get back into my own house, if you don't mind. Now, come on.

ROSEMARY (*producing the key from her bag*): Here.

LUCY: Rosemary, don't you dare give it to him.

TERRY: Eh?

ROSEMARY: What?

LUCY: Not until he apologizes.

TERRY: Rosie, give me the key.

LUCY: No, Rosemary. I'll take it. Give it to me.

TERRY: Rosie.

LUCY: Rosemary.

ROSEMARY (*torn*): Er . . .

LUCY (*very fiercely*): Rosemary, will you give me that key at once.

ROSEMARY *gives* LUCY *the key.* TERRY *regards* LUCY.

TERRY: Would you mind most awfully giving me the key to my own front door?

LUCY: Certainly.

TERRY: Thank you so much.

LUCY: Just as soon as you've apologized to Rosemary.

TERRY: I've said, I'm not apologizing to anyone.

LUCY: Then you're not having the key.

TERRY: Now listen, I've got a day's work to do tomorrow. I'm damned if I'm going to start playing games with some frustrated nutter* . . .

ROSEMARY: Terry . . .

LUCY: Take no notice of him, Rosemary, he's just showing off.*

TERRY: Are you going to give me that key or not?

LUCY: Not until you apologize.

TERRY: All right. I'll have to come and take it off you, won't I?

LUCY: You try. You just dare try, my boy.

TERRY: All right. (*He moves towards* LUCY.)

ROSEMARY: Terry . . .

LUCY: Just you try and see what happens.

TERRY (*halted* by her tone; uncertainly*): I'm not joking.

LUCY: Neither am I.

TERRY: Look, I don't want to ... Just give me the key, there's a
good ...

LUCY: Not until you apologize to Rosemary.

TERRY: Oh, for the love of ... All right (*To* ROSEMARY)
Sorry.

LUCY: Say it nicely.

TERRY: I'm very sorry, Rosie. Now give us the key, for
God's sake.

LUCY: When you've drunk your milk. Sit down and drink your
milk.

TERRY: Oh, blimey* ... (*He sits.*)

LUCY: That's better.

TERRY: I hate milk.

LUCY: Drink it up.

> TERRY *scowls* and picks up the glass.* ROSEMARY, *unseen by*
> LUCY, *sticks her tongue out at him.* TERRY *bangs down his*
> *glass and moves as if to hit her.*

Terry!

TERRY: She stuck her tongue out at me.

LUCY: Sit still.

TERRY: But she ...

LUCY: Sit!

> TERRY *sits scowling.* ROSEMARY *smirks* at him smugly.* *

(*Seeing her*): And don't do that, Rosemary. If the wind
changes, you'll get stuck like it. And sit up straight and
don't slouch.*

> ROSEMARY *does so.*

TERRY (*taking a sip of the milk*): This is horrible.

> *Silence. He takes another sip.*

It's warm.

> *Silence. Another sip.*

TERRY: There's a football international on television, you
know.

LUCY: Not until you've drunk that up, there isn't. Come on,
Rosemary. Help Terry to drink it. 'Georgie Porgie* Pudding
and Pie, Kissed the girls and ...?'

ROSEMARY: 'Made them cry.'

LUCY: Good.

ROSEMARY *(speaking* ⎱ . 'When the boys came out to play,
LUCY   *together* ⎰   Georgie Porgie ran away.'

TERRY (*finishing his glass with a giant swallow.*): All gone.
   (*He wipes his mouth.*)

LUCY: Good boy.

TERRY: Can I have the key now, please?

LUCY: Here you are.

   TERRY *goes to take it.*

   What do you say?

TERRY: Thank you.

LUCY: All right. Off you go, both of you.

ROSEMARY (*kissing her on the cheek*): Night night.

LUCY: Night night, dear. Night night, Terry.

TERRY (*kissing Lucy likewise*): Night night.

LUCY: Sleep tight.

TERRY: Hope the bugs don't bite.*

LUCY: Hold Rosemary's hand, Terry.

   ROSEMARY *and* TERRY *hold hands.*

   See her home safely.

TERRY: Night.

ROSEMARY: Night.

LUCY: Night night.

   TERRY *and* ROSEMARY *go off hand in hand.* LUCY *blows
   kisses.*

   (*With a sigh*): Blooming* kids. Honestly.

Glossary

The meanings given below are those which the words and phrases have as they occur in the play.

Page
161 *dinkie* (baby talk):   drink.
chimes: bells.
toothipegs (baby talk):   teeth.
botty (baby talk): bottom.
frail: weak, feeble.
mousey-looking: timid and a bit dull-looking.
162 *option*:   freedom of choice.
attire: clothing.
163 *play-pen*:   small area enclosed by bars where a young child can play safely.
transfer charge call: a telephone call in which the receiver pays for the call.
Middlesbrough: an industrial town in the north of England.
won't sleep a wink: won't sleep at all.
164 *pop round*:   pay a very short visit.
warmly: in a sentimental voice (still thinking of Nicholas as the baby).
hang on: wait.
gingerly: cautiously, as though looking out for danger.
165 *pudgy*:   short and fat.
sotto voce (Italian):   in a soft voice so as not to be heard by everyone.
166 *choccy bics* (baby talk):   chocolate biscuits.
nappies: cloth garments worn around a baby's bottom and between its legs.
167 *on the nose* (coll.):   exactly at.
roving at will: moving around where and when he wants.
munches: eats with strong mouth movements, eats noisily.
168 *idle loafer*:   lazy person.
touchy: too sensitive, easily annoyed.
Niggle: find fault.
169 *filthy mood*:   very bad temper.
drains: completely empties.
distraught: very unhappy.
170 *whining*:   complaining in an unpleasant sounding way.
171 *sulk*:   be silently annoyed over a small matter.
lamely: weakly.

172   *nutter* (sl.):   madwoman.
    showing off: trying to get others to think he is important.
    halted: stopped.
173   *blimey* (Br.E., sl.):   an expression of protest.
    scowls: looks angrily.
    smirks: smiles in a silly, self-satisfied way.
    smugly: with self-satisfaction.
    slouch: sit low down in a chair in a tired way.
    Georgie Porgie etc.:   a British children's song.
174   *Night night ... don't bite*:   a children's bedtime rhyme.
    Blooming (sl.):   a mild form of 'bloody'.

Questions

> OUTLINE TO QUESTIONS
>
> 1.   characterization: Lucy
> 2.   characterization: Terry and Rosemary
> 3.   genre/characterization: Lucy, Terry, Rosemary
> 4.   themes

1.   Why does Lucy behave in the way she does?

   (a)   Why does Lucy wear a dressing gown and slippers in the middle of the day (p. 161)?
   (b)   Why does Lucy say 'I haven't much option'. (p. 162) about looking after her children?
   (c)   Why might someone in Lucy's situation talk to everyone as though they were a child?
   (d)   Why is Lucy's husband not often home?
   (e)   Why does Lucy not answer her husband's telephone call (p. 164)?
   (f)   Terry talks to Lucy about the 'natural way of life' for a man and a woman (p. 167). Why does Rosemary try and stop him talking?
   (g)   Terry says 'You can't put a man in a cage. You try to do that, you've lost him', to which Lucy replies 'That can apply to women, too, surely?' (p. 167). Why does she say this?

2. What sort of marriage do Terry and Rosemary have?

   (a) Where, for Terry, is a woman's place (p. 167)? Does his wife agree?
   (b) What different reasons do Terry and Rosemary have for finding Lucy 'odd' (p. 168)?
   (c) What do these reasons tell us about their attitudes?
   (d) What complaints do Terry and Rosemary have about each other (pp. 167–170)?

3. In what ways is *Mother Figure* both realistic and comically absurd?

   (a) Where is the first indication that Lucy treats Rosemary as a child (p. 165)?
   (b) Does this come as a surprise or is the audience already prepared for Lucy's behaviour?
   (c) After this point does Lucy at any time treat Terry and Rosemary as adults?
   (d) In what ways do Terry and Rosemary act towards each other like spoilt children? Is such behaviour between married people realistically possible?
   (e) At what point does Terry accept Lucy as a 'mother figure' and begin to act like a well-behaved child (p. 173)? Is this change in Terry's behaviour realistically possible?

4. Which of these points do you think the play shows? Give reasons. Are some of these ideas more important in the play than others? Rank them in order of importance (1 = the most significant theme, 5 = the least significant).

   (a) Lucy behaves as she does because she is at home with children all day.
   (b) Lucy behaves as she does because her husband escapes from his responsibilities as a father.
   (c) Adults can become child-like when treated as children.
   (d) Problems between married couples may come from spending too much time together.
   (e) Adults act childishly at times.

Drama Activities

Choose *ONE* of these scenes. Prepare a dialogue in pairs and practise it within your own groups. It may then be shown to the whole group.

1. The conversation between Terry and Rosemary when they get home.

2. The conversation between Harry and Lucy after Harry finally gets home.

3. A scene in a bar where Harry talks to a male friend about the problems he is having with his wife.

4. A scene in which a successful businessman in his thirties goes to his mother's and is treated as though he were a small boy.

Staging

Where would you place the two doors, the coffee table, the sofa or chairs, the play-pen etc.

Rosemary is described as *'mousey-looking'* (p. 161). What sort of clothing should she wear?

How would you suggest timidity in Rosemary's manner when she comes in (p. 161)?

How confident would you make Terry seem when he comes in (p. 165)?

Where would he act uncertainly?

After Rosemary comes in, at what point does Lucy change her voice to a tone used for talking to children?

What tone of voice and physical gestures would you use to make Terry and Rosemary appear child-like at the end of the play (pp. 173—174)?

Edward Albee

Edward Albee, one of America's best-known and most respected dramatists, was born in Washington D.C. in 1928. At the age of two weeks he was adopted by Reed Albee, the millionaire owner of a chain of theatres, and his wife, Frances, who was 23 years younger than her husband and the dominant member of the family. It is possible that Albee's criticism of self-satisfied family life in such early plays as *The Sandbox* (1958), *The American Dream* (1960) and *Who's Afraid of Virginia Wolf?* (1962) come from personal experience as the adopted child of a rich family, though Albee's plays go beyond attacks on the family to a radical criticism of many aspects of American life.

Albee has been considered by some as a dramatist of the 'Theatre of the Absurd', and it is true that some of his plays, such as *The Zoo Story* (1958), his first important play, and the one-act plays that followed — *The Death of Bessie Smith* (1959), *The Sandbox* and *The American Dream* — all owe something stylistically to the masters of absurd drama, Eugene Ionesco and Samuel Beckett.

Among Albee's more recent plays are *Quotations from Chairman Mao Tse Tung* (1968) and *All Over* (1970).

THE PLAY

In 1959, Grandma Cotta, Albee's grandmother on his mother's side, died. *The Sandbox*, a personal favourite of Albee's, is dedicated to this old lady, to whom he felt particularly close. In *The Sandbox*, Grandma is dying, though she still has a bright mind and a lively tongue. Mommy and Daddy, meanwhile, prepare for her death — with a lot of sentiment but with no real feeling.

CHARACTERS

THE YOUNG MAN (25): a good-looking, well-built boy in a bathing suit.
MOMMY (55): a well-dressed, imposing* woman.
DADDY (60): a small man; gray, thin.
GRANDMA (86): a tiny, wizened* woman with bright eyes.
THE MUSICIAN (non-speaking): no particular age, but young would be nice.

SPELLING NOTE

The spelling in this play is American.

THE SANDBOX*

Note: *When, in the course of the play,* MOMMY *and* DADDY *call each other by these names, there should be no suggestion of regionalism. These names are of empty affection and point up the pre-senility* and vacuity* of their characters.*

The Scene: *A bare stage, with only the following: near the footlights,* far stage-right,* two simple chairs set side by side, facing the audience; near the footlights, far stage-left, a chair facing stage-right with a music stand before it; farther back, and stage-center, slightly elevated and raked,* a large child's sandbox with a toy pail* and shovel;* the background is the sky, which alters from brightest day to deepest night.*

At the beginning, it is brightest day; the YOUNG MAN *is alone on stage, to the rear of the sandbox, and to one side. He is doing calisthenics;* he does calisthenics until quite at the very end of the play. These calisthenics, employing the arms only, should suggest the beating and fluttering of wings. The* YOUNG MAN *is, after all, the Angel of Death.*

MOMMY *and* DADDY *enter from stage-left,* MOMMY *first.*

MOMMY *(motioning to* DADDY*):* Well, here we are; this is the beach.

DADDY *(whining*):* I'm cold.

MOMMY *(dismissing him with a little laugh):* Don't be silly; it's as warm as toast. Look at that nice young man over there: *he* doesn't think it's cold. *(Waves to the* YOUNG MAN.) Hello.

YOUNG MAN *(with an endearing* smile):* Hi!

MOMMY *(looking about):* This will do perfectly ... don't you think so, Daddy? There's sand there ... and the water beyond. What do you think, Daddy?

DADDY *(vaguely):* Whatever you say, Mommy.

MOMMY *(with the same little laugh):* Well, of course ... whatever I say. Then, it's settled, is it?

181

DADDY (*shrugs**): She's *your* mother, not mine.

MOMMY: *I* know she's my mother. What do you take me for?*
(*A pause.*) All right, now; let's get on with it. (*She shouts into the wings, stage-left*) You! Out there! You can come in now.

The MUSICIAN *enters, seats himself in the chair, stage-left, places music on the music stand, is ready to play.* MOMMY *nods approvingly.*

MOMMY: Very nice; very nice. Are you ready, Daddy? Let's go get Grandma.

DADDY: Whatever you say, Mommy.

MOMMY (*leading the way out, stage-left*): Of course, whatever I say. (*To the* MUSICIAN) You can begin now.

The MUSICIAN *begins playing;* MOMMY *and* DADDY *exit; the* MUSICIAN, *all the while playing, nods to the* YOUNG MAN.

YOUNG MAN (*with the same endearing smile*): Hi!

After a moment, MOMMY *and* DADDY *re-enter, carrying* GRANDMA. *She is borne in by their hands under her armpits; she is quite rigid; her legs are drawn up; her feet do not touch the ground; the expression on her ancient face is that of puzzlement and fear.*

DADDY: Where do we put her?

MOMMY (*The same little laugh.*): Wherever I say, of course. Let me see ... well ... all right, over there ... in the sandbox. (*Pause.*) Well, what are you waiting for, Daddy? ... The sandbox!

Together they carry GRANDMA *over to the sandbox and more or less dump* her in.*

GRANDMA (*righting herself to a sitting position; her voice a cross between a baby's laugh and cry*): Ahhhhhh! Graaaaa!

DADDY (*dusting himself*): What do we do now?

MOMMY (*to the* MUSICIAN): You can stop now.

The MUSICIAN *stops.*

(*Back to* DADDY): What do you mean, what do we do now? We go over there and sit down, of course. (*To the* YOUNG MAN) Hello there.

YOUNG MAN (*again smiling*): Hi!

MOMMY *and* DADDY *move to the chairs, stage-right, and sit down. A pause.*

GRANDMA (*same as before*): Ahhhhhh! Ah-haaaaaa! Graa-aaaa!

DADDY: Do you think . . . do you think she's . . . comfortable?

MOMMY (*impatiently*): How would I know?

DADDY (*Pause.*): What do we do now?

MOMMY (*as if remembering*): We . . . wait. We . . . sit here . . . and we wait . . . that's what we do.

DADDY (*after a pause*): Shall we talk to each other?

MOMMY (*with that little laugh; picking something off her dress*): Well, you can talk, if you want to . . . if you can think of anything to say . . . if you can think of anything *new*.

DADDY (*Thinks.*): No . . . I suppose not.

MOMMY (*with a triumphant laugh*): Of course not!

GRANDMA (*banging the toy shovel against the pail*): Haaaaaa! Ahhaaaaaa!

MOMMY (*out over the audience*): Be quiet, Grandma . . . just be quiet, and wait.

GRANDMA *throws a shovelful of sand at* MOMMY.

MOMMY (*still out over the audience*): She's throwing sand at me! You stop that, Grandma; you stop throwing sand at Mommy! (*To* DADDY) She's throwing sand at me.

DADDY *looks around at* GRANDMA, *who screams at him.*

GRANDMA: GRAAAAAA!

MOMMY: Don't look at her. Just . . . sit here . . . be very still . . . and wait. (*To the* MUSICIAN) You . . . uh . . . you go ahead and do whatever it is you do.

The MUSICIAN *plays.*

MOMMY *and* DADDY *are fixed, staring out beyond the audience.* GRANDMA *looks at them, looks at the* MUSICIAN, *looks at the sandbox, throws down the shovel.*

GRANDMA: Ah-haaaaaa! Graaaaaa! (*Looks for reaction; gets none. Now . . . directly to the audience*) Honestly! What a way to treat an old woman! Drag her out of the house . . . stick her in a car . . . bring her out here from the city . . . dump her in a pile of sand . . . and leave her here to set.* I'm

eighty-six years old! I was married when I was seventeen.
To a farmer. He died when I was thirty. (*To the* MUSICIAN)
Will you stop that, please?

The MUSICIAN *stops playing.*

I'm a feeble old woman ... how do you expect anybody to
hear me over that peep! peep! peep! (*To herself*) There's no
respect around here. (*To the* YOUNG MAN) There's no respect
around here!

YOUNG MAN   (*same smile*):   Hi!

GRANDMA   (*after a pause, a mild double-take,* * *continues, to the
    audience*):   My husband died when I was thirty (*indicates*
    MOMMY) and I had to raise that big cow over there all by my
    lonesome. You can imagine what *that* was like. Lordy! (*To
    the* YOUNG MAN) Where'd they get *you*?

YOUNG MAN: Oh ... I've been around for a while.

GRANDMA: I'll bet you have! Heh, heh, heh. Will you look at
    you!

YOUNG MAN   (*flexing* * *his muscles*):   Isn't that something?
    (*Continues his calisthenics.*)

GRANDMA: Boy, oh boy; I'll say. Pretty good.

YOUNG MAN   (*sweetly*):   I'll say.

GRANDMA: Where ya from?

YOUNG MAN: Southern California.

GRANDMA   (*nodding*):   Figgers;* figgers. What's your name,
    honey?

YOUNG MAN: I don't know. . . .

GRANDMA   (*to the audience*):   Bright, too!

YOUNG MAN: I mean ... I mean, they haven't given me one yet
    ... the studio* ...

GRANDMA   (*giving him the once-over*):   You don't say ... you
    don't say. Well ... uh, I've got to talk some more ... don't
    you go 'way.

YOUNG MAN: Oh, no.

GRANDMA   (*turning her attention back to the audience*):   Fine;
    fine. (*Then, once more, back to the* YOUNG MAN) You're ...
    you're an actor, huh?

YOUNG MAN   (*beaming**):   Yes, I am.

GRANDMA   (*to the audience again; shrugs*):   I'm smart that
    way. *Anyhow*, I had to raise ... *that* over there all by my
    lonesome; and what's next to her there ... that's what she

married. Rich? I tell you ... money, money, money. They took me off the *farm* ... which was real decent of them ... and they moved me into the big town house with *them* ... fixed a nice place for me under the stove ... gave me an army blanket ... and my own dish ... my very own dish! So, what have I got to complain about? Nothing, of course. I'm not complaining. (*She looks up at the sky, shouts to someone off stage*) Shouldn't it be getting dark now, dear?

The lights dim; night comes on. The MUSICIAN *begins to play; it becomes deepest night. There are spots* on all the players, including the* YOUNG MAN, *who is, of course, continuing his calisthenics.*

DADDY (*stirring*):* It's nighttime.

MOMMY: Shhhh. Be still ... wait.

DADDY (*whining*): It's so hot.

MOMMY: Shhhhhh. Be still ... wait.

GRANDMA (*to herself*): That's better. Night. (*To the* MUSICIAN) Honey, do you play all through this part?

The MUSICIAN *nods.*

Well, keep it nice and soft; that's a good boy.

The MUSICIAN *nods again; plays softly.*

That's nice.

There is an off-stage rumble.*

DADDY (*starting**): What was that?

MOMMY (*beginning to weep*): It was nothing.

DADDY: It was ... it was ... thunder ... or a wave breaking ... or something.

MOMMY (*whispering, through her tears*): It was an off-stage rumble ... and you know what *that* means....

DADDY: I forget....

MOMMY (*barely able to talk*): It means the time has come for poor Grandma ... and I can't bear it!*

DADDY (*vacantly*): I ... I suppose you've got to be brave.

GRANDMA (*mocking**): That's right, kid; be brave. You'll bear up; you'll get over it.

Another off-stage rumble ... louder.

MOMMY: Ohhhhhhhhhh ... poor Grandma ... poor Grandma. . . .

GRANDMA (*to* MOMMY): I'm fine! I'm all right! It hasn't happened yet!

A violent off-stage rumble. All the lights go out, save the spot on the YOUNG MAN; *the* MUSICIAN *stops playing.*

MOMMY: Ohhhhhhhhhh ... Ohhhhhhhhhh ...

Silence.

GRANDMA: Don't put the lights up yet ... I'm not ready; I'm not quite ready. (*Silence.*) All right, dear ... I'm about done.

The lights come up again, to brightest day; the MUSICIAN *begins to play.* GRANDMA *is discovered, still in the sandbox, lying on her side, propped up* on an elbow, half covered, busily shoveling sand over herself.*

(*Muttering*): I don't know how I'm supposed to do anything with this goddam toy shovel. . . .

DADDY: Mommy! It's daylight!

MOMMY (*brightly*): So it is! Well! Our long night is over. We must put away our tears, take off our mourning* ... and face the future. It's our duty.

GRANDMA (*still shoveling; mimicking**): ... take off our mourning ... face the future ... Lordy!

MOMMY *and* DADDY *rise, stretch.* MOMMY *waves to the* YOUNG MAN.

YOUNG MAN (*with that smile*): Hi!

GRANDMA *plays dead.* (!) MOMMY *and* DADDY *go over to look at her; she is a little more than half buried in the sand; the toy shovel is in her hands, which are crossed on her breast.*

MOMMY (*before the sandbox; shaking her head*): Lovely! It's ... it's hard to be sad ... she looks ... so happy. (*With pride and conviction*) It pays to do things well. (*To the* MUSICIAN) All right, you can stop now, if you want to. I mean, stay around for a swim, or something; it's all right with us. (*She sighs heavily.*) Well, Daddy ... off we go.

DADDY: Brave Mommy!

MOMMY: Brave Daddy!

They exit, stage-left.

GRANDMA *(after they leave; lying quite still)*:   It pays to do things well.... Boy, oh boy! *(She tries to sit up)* ... well, kids ... *(but she finds she can't)* ... I ... I can't get up. I ... I can't move....

The YOUNG MAN *stops his calisthenics, nods to the MUSICIAN, walks over to* GRANDMA, *kneels down by the sandbox.*

GRANDMA: I ... can't move....

YOUNG MAN: Shhhhh ... be very still....

GRANDMA: I ... I can't move....

YOUNG MAN: Uh ... ma'am; I ... I have a line here.

GRANDMA: Oh, I'm sorry, sweetie; you go right ahead.

YOUNG MAN: I am ... uh ...

GRANDMA: Take your time, dear.

YOUNG MAN *(prepares; delivers the line like a real amateur)*:   I am the Angel of Death. I am ... uh ... I am come for you.

GRANDMA: What ... wha ... *(Then, with resignation*)* ... ohhhh ... ohhhh, I see.

The YOUNG MAN *bends over, kisses* GRANDMA *gently on the forehead.*

GRANDMA *(her eyes closed, her hands folded on her breast again, the shovel between her hands, a sweet smile on her face)*:   Well ... that was very nice, dear....

YOUNG MAN *(still kneeling)*:   Shhhhhh ... be still....

GRANDMA: What I meant was ... you did that very well, dear ...

YOUNG MAN *(blushing)*:   ... oh ...

GRANDMA: No; I mean it. You've got that ... you've got a quality.

YOUNG MAN *(with his endearing smile)*:   Oh ... thank you; thank you very much ... ma'am.

GRANDMA *(slowly; softly — as the* YOUNG MAN *puts his hands on top of* GRANDMA'S*)*:   You're ... you're welcome ... dear.

Tableau.* The MUSICIAN *continues to play as the curtain slowly comes down.*

CURTAIN

Glossary

The meanings given below are those which the words and phrases have as they occur in the play.

Page
181   *sandbox*:   enclosure filled with sand for children to play in.
imposing: impressive in appearance.
wizened: dried up, with lines in the skin.
pre-senility: weakness of mind that will get worse with increasing age.
vacuity: lack of imagination or ideas.
footlights: lights at the front of the stage which shine on the actors.
far stage-right: to the right of an actor facing the theatre seats, at the edge of the stage.
raked: sloped upwards at the back (so the audience can see it).
pail: small bucket.
shovel: small tool, like a spade, for lifting sand and other loose material.
calisthenics: exercises to develop a healthy and beautiful body.
whining: in a complaining voice.
endearing: attractive, lovable.
182   *shrugs*:   raises his shoulders, expressing doubt or lack of interest.
What do you take me for: meaning 'I am not uncaring even if you think I am.'
dump: drop carelessly.
183   *set*:   (Am.E.dial.): sit
184   *double-take*:   a delayed movement of surprise, producing a comic effect.
flexing: contracting, moving in and out.
Figgers   (Incorrect spelling of 'figures', to show pronunciation in Am.E.): that is what I expected.
studio: film company.
beaming: smiling broadly.
185   *spots*:   bright round areas of light.
stirring: moving after being still.
rumble: deep, continuous rolling sound, like thunder.
starting: moving quickly as if suddenly surprised.
I can't bear it: it's too much for me.
vacantly: without actively thinking, absently.

mocking: imitating in a scornful way.
186 *propped up*:   supported.
mourning: dark clothes worn as a conventional sign of grief after a death.
mimicking: imitating, talking in a similar voice.
187 *resignation*:   acceptance.
Tableau: pause in which the actors do not move or speak.

Questions

OUTLINE TO QUESTIONS
1. theme/characterization: Mommy and Daddy
2. theme/characterization: Grandma, Mommy
3. theme/characterization: Grandma, Young Man
4. genre/characterization: Grandma, Mommy, Young Man

1. What point is Albee making through the relationship of Mommy and Daddy?

   (a) When Mommy and Daddy appear on the stage (pp. 181—182), who is obviously the more dominant person? Give examples of dominance and weakness.
   (b) Mommy says 'Then, it's settled, is it?' (p. 181). What has been settled? Has Daddy made any decision in the matter?
   (c) How does Mommy treat Daddy when he says 'Shall we talk to each other?' (p. 183)? Why does she treat him like this?
   (d) Why do they call each other Mommy and Daddy instead of using first names (p. 181)?
   (e) Why do they call each other 'brave' (p. 186)?

2. What attitudes to death and old people are shown in *The Sandbox*?

   (a) How is Grandma treated when she is brought in by Mommy and Daddy (p. 182)?
   (b) Why does Grandma at first act childishly (pp. 182—183) but afterwards behave intelligently and humorously?
   (c) In what way does Mommy tell the Musician to come in (p. 182)?

(d) Why is the Musician told to start play just before Grandma is brought in (p. 182), and told to stop after she has apparently died (p. 186)? What is his function?

(e) What does Mommy mean when she says 'It pays to do things well.' (p. 186) after Grandma has apparently died?

(f) At three points in the play (p. 185, p. 186, p. 187) Grandma mockingly repeats the words that Mommy and Daddy use. What types of attitude and emotion are being satirized here?

3. What does the relationship between Grandma and the Young Man add to the play?

(a) Albee tells the reader that the Young Man represents the Angel of Death (p. 181). When would the audience in the theatre realize this? When does Grandma realize it?

(b) What is there about the Angel of Death (his intelligence, his job, Grandma's attitude to him, pp. 184—185) that stops us from thinking of him in a sentimental way?

(c) Considering that the Young Man represents the Angel of Death, what sort of ideas and feelings are suggested by the following lines?

> GRANDMA: 'I've got to talk some more . . . don't you go away.
> YOUNG MAN: Oh, no.' (p. 184)
> GRANDMA (*as the* YOUNG MAN *put his hands on top of* GRANDMA'S): 'You're . . . you're welcome . . . dear.' (p. 187)

4. In what ways and why does *The Sandbox* remind the audience that they are watching a play?

(a) Where is the scene set and who tells us this (p. 181)?

(b) In what ways does Mommy treat the Musician like a director telling an actor what to do (p. 182, p. 186)?

(c) What words show that Mommy sees herself as if she were a tragic actress (p. 186)? Why does she see herself like this?

(d) What does the '*off-stage rumble*' mean (p. 185)? How is it that Mommy knows its meaning?

(e) Like Mommy, the Young Man is an actor with a part to play. What is that part, and how does Grandma encourage him to play it (p. 187)?

(f) The lighting goes from brightest day (p. 181) to deepest night (p. 185) and back to brightest day again (p. 186).

What events in the play do these lighting changes accompany?

(g) What does Grandma say that emphasizes the fact that the lighting changes are a deliberate theatrical device (p. 185)?

Drama Activities

Choose *ONE* of these scenes. Prepare and practise it in groups of three (2. may be done in pairs). Scenes 1., 2. and 3. may be combined to form a continuous class performance.

1. A scene from Grandma's life with Mommy and Daddy at their big town house (see p. 185).

2. A scene before *The Sandbox* starts. Mommy and Daddy are sitting in their kitchen planning the arrangements for Grandma's meeting with the Angel of Death. The scene could also include a conversation with the Musician (over the phone, perhaps) about the arrangements.

> USEFUL PHRASES FOR 2
>
> *Mommy*
>
> What do you think . . .?
> Of course, whatever I say . . .
> Let me see . . .
> What do you mean, what do we do then?
> We could . . . of course.
> Of course not!
>
> *Daddy*
>
> Whatever you say . . .
> What do we do then?
> Shall we . . .?
> No, . . . I suppose not.

3. An alternative ending to *The Sandbox*. After the '*off-stage rumble*' (p. 185) and the beginning of another day, Mommy and Daddy are surprised to find that Grandma has not died in the night.

Staging

Draw a plan of the stage and its furniture and property. Mark on the entrances and movements of all the characters.

What are Mommy and Daddy and the Musician doing whilst Grandma and the Young Man are playing their scene (pp. 184—185)?

Could the play be performed effectively without lighting? What alternative arrangements would you make?

What sort of musical instrument and music would it be appropriate for the Musician to play?

★　　★　　★　　★　　★

Mother Figure and The Sandbox: comparative questions

1. Absurdity may be defined as 'against reason or common sense, funny because false, foolish or impossible'. Which play do you think is more absurdist? Why? Are the characters of one play more realistic than those of the other?

2. Compare the reasons why some people treat others as children in the two plays.

3. Do you find one play more amusing than the other? Why?

4. Is one play more critical of certain aspects of relationships than the other?